PARENTING YOUR CHILD

Forming Lifelong Friendships with your Children

Dr. Ron Hitchcock

FEATURING

The Parenting Adult Children Model

Nurture	Values	Mutuality	Interdependence
0–6 years	7–12 years	13–18 years	19–27 years

Published by Life In Motion Resources
Westerville, Ohio
http://www.lifeinmotionresources.com
Email: ron@lifeinmotionresources.com

ISBN-13: 978-1514237717

ISBN-10: 1514237717

Parenting your Children into Adulthood

*Forming Lifelong Friendships
with your Children*

Contents

Introduction

The idea of family ministry was deposited into my heart in a dramatic way. I was praying for the teens in my church when the Lord spoke something into my heart:

"I am going to frustrate the hand of youth ministry and drive it back to where it belongs, the home."

These words changed everything about my life and ministry. My wife and I had made a commitment to serve the local church as youth pastors and were enjoying the fruit of equipping teens to follow the Lord as leaders in the church.

The first step toward family ministry was to come alongside of parents as the primary voices of discipleship in their children's lives. Most of the parents I worked with wanted to be actively engaged in the discipleship process of their children. However, most resources defined discipleship as Bible memorization and prayer. These disciplines are essential to Christian maturity. However, children need a relational model of discipleship.

I developed *Journey to Oneness* to equip married couples to model spiritual identity, friendship, validation, sacrificial love and covenant vows to their children. The best gift parents can give their children is a healthy model of relationships to emulate in their lives as future spouses and parents.

The second step was developing the Parenting Adult Children (PAC) Model. *Parenting Your Children into Adulthood* equips parents to deposit the essential characteristics of nurture, values, mutuality, and interdependence into children's lives. These characteristics prepare children to become healthy spouses and parents.

Many people participated in developing the idea behind this book: Judy Nieme, Carol McClure, Gloria Redding, Jewell Mongeau, Michelle Damron, my Marriage & Family Life staff at Vineyard Columbus and, most of all my wife, Barbara, and our children, Veronica and Ron Jr. My wife and I had to practice everything on our children and, as a result, we are a close family and friends.

My hope is that parents will experience God's empowerment, blessings and peace as they raise their children as brothers and sisters in Christ and life-long friends.

CHAPTER 1

The Journey

I hope that *Parenting Your Children into Adulthood* will encourage all moms and dads to embrace the amazing journey that comes with loving your children. Too often parents seek to be successful rather than faithful when it comes to parenting. The first lesson parents must learn is that faithful parents are not born but formed. Parenting forms you into faithful stewards of God's precious children.

Many books are written to help parents understand their children's behavioral, emotional and physical development. I hope to bring my readers a different perspective on parenting. Faithful parenting is not accomplished by applying the latest research, even though such information can be very helpful.

Parenting is a divine responsibility that requires parents to look beyond themselves in order to establish and cultivate sacrificial love in their children's lives. *Parenting Your Children into Adulthood* is written for all parents and is applicable to all family types.

God's Plan for Families

The first parent was God. His first children, Adam and Eve, were given responsibilities to work together as caretakers in the Garden of Eden. The purpose for their lives included raising children, "be fruitful and multiply ..." (Genesis 1:22 NASB), and serving each other. Even though Adam and Eve rebelled against God, his purposes for families did not change. God's plan for families would set humanity on a course of reconciliation with their heavenly Father.

The home is the best environment for children to experience forgiveness, grace, mercy and justice from their heavenly Father. The purpose of family life was to experience these attributes in every home. However, sin has been very destructive to family relationships. The Bible tells many stories of how sin devastated family relationships and how God restored family members through his provision of reconciliation.

Thousands of years later, family life was at the forefront of God's purpose and plan as humanity and divinity dwelled together. His only begotten Son, Jesus, was born into a human family. The Savior of the world grew up in a family, where he experienced all of the blessings of loving relationships, as well as the sufferings associated with the consequences of living in a fallen world. I believe that, as Jesus lived within a normal family, happiness and heartache played an important role in preparing him to be Savior of the world.

Families continue to be mankind's best chance of developing relationships that are based upon faith, unconditional love and divine forgiveness. The family is the one constant in every nation, kingdom, and community.

In my opinion, parent and child relationships continue to represent the best opportunity for children to receive the benefits of reconciliation between God and humankind. Parents are responsible to demonstrate reconciled relationships with God to their children. The home is an environment that invites children into a restored humanity, allowing them to discover God's love, personally and in the context of family relationships.

Attacks on the Family

Christians must be aware that resistance from the kingdom of darkness (emphasis mine) always follows an outpouring of grace and redemption upon humankind. Parenting has come under great attack, not only from our culture and society, but also from the spiritual realms.

The Bible records these attempts to separate children and parents from each other in Exodus 1:15–16 and Matthew 2:7–12. The first account is an attempt to decrease the number of male children being born; the second is an attempt to kill the Messiah (Jesus). Fortunately, God was faithful to ensure that Moses and Jesus were born safely born into the world. These plans were thwarted by God, and faithful men and women who were obedient to his Lordship.

Many cultures and societies continued to treat children as property rather being guardians of life and mentors of redemption. Unfortunately, these types of tactics against families, as described in the Scriptures, did not cease in the first century. New strategies include disrupting the stability of family life.

Many children grow up in two or more households over their lifetimes, and up to thirty percent of children grow up in single parent homes (Mather, 2010). The instability of family life impedes children from experiencing a comprehensive imprint of redemption and reconciliation in their homes. As a result, the spiritual identities of both parents and children suffer.

The family was intended to be the safest and best environment for children to experience the benefits of grace, redemption and spiritual development. Many parents need to rediscover God's purposes for their families in order to combat the loss of stability due to the cultural acceptance of divorce, fatherlessness or never-married parents.

Fortunately, any home where Jesus is Lord can model sacrificial love and reconciliation. Not every home will have the blessing of two parents raising their biological children. God's provision and purpose for family life extends to everyone, including single parent, stepfamily and extended families.

Recapturing God's Heart for Family

One of the first steps in recapturing God's heart for families is to ask good questions. The wrong question is: "When are my children going to change or act more like I imagined?" The right question is: "What changes does God want to make in me as parent and spiritual leader of my children?"

The first question puts the emphasis of change upon children. Parents need to assess why they want their children to change. Perhaps their children are making life chaotic for them. While this may be true, as parents we must embrace and validate our children just as they are.

Parents are change agents in their children's lives as they model truth and righteousness in a culture that values relevant truth rather that biblical truth. The second question allows parents to form partnerships with God as change agents in their children's lives.

Divine Partnerships

God's love, grace, mercy, and justice transforms a self-centered people into sacrificial servants who extends these life changing attributes to family members, friends, neighbors and coworkers. These attributes are limitless, so Christians are continually growing in depth and understanding of perfect love.

Parents are in progressive states of transformation throughout their lives. This allows their children to experience increasing measures of grace, mercy, love and justice as they advance in age and maturity. Parents need to let go of the idea that they can parent in ways that seem best to them. They are in divine partnerships with God to reveal Christ-like character to their children.

Parents must avoid the common mistake of ignoring their own spiritual development in order to complete everything on his or her to do list. All parents will discover that children need more than what they alone are capable of giving to them. Married parents will find that investing in their marriage relationship will add strength and resources that can be extended to their children. Single parents do not have the resource of a spouse. However, they can learn to partner with grandparents, teachers and coaches whenever possible.

Parents need to be recipients of God's love, patience, grace and justice in order to extend these attributes toward their children. When parents do not regularly receive grace and strength from God, they may develop hardened hearts toward their children, due to all of the sacrifices that could never be rewarded in this life.

Parents can become disheartened at giving so much time, energy and resources away to their children, especially, when family life is chaotic rather than harmonious or structured. All parents must remember that parenting requires more time, energy, wisdom, or patience than they have the capacity to give on a daily basis. Parenting requires moms and dads to seek help from the Holy Spirit who refreshes them with love, patience, endurance and wisdom.

Abbey and Pete have been married for seven years. They have two daughters, ages five and three. Abbey says:

> *"I thought I was a patient person until I had my kids. Parenting my children allowed me to recognize my perfectionism. I wanted my children to look and act a certain way, especially in public. When things did not work out my way, I began to desire my old life. A life that was not unpredictable or messy. I never thought my children would say, 'No,' to me in front of people in the mall or argue with me in a checkout line at the grocery store. I also struggled when parenting responsibilities required me to sacrifice time and attention that was once dedicated toward my career and life goals. I had to learn how to count the time and energy that was redirected toward my children as sacrificial love. I would often ask myself the question: 'When will it be time for me?!'"*

Abbey quickly recognized that parenting responsibilities did not fit neatly into her pre-parent lifestyle. Parenting requires changes in lifestyle priorities, such as everything being tidy or clean, or always being on time. Her story affirms that all parents need to open up their hearts to God, who is their source of sacrificial love, in order to have reasonable expectations of family life.

Abbey represents parents who work at home or in the corporate world. As a couple they need to embrace the tensions between what worked best for her and Pete before children and how parenting responsibilities impacts their personal lives and relationship.

Abbey describes her mom in this way:

"My mom always prioritized her time with us. We felt affirmed by her presence, so I knew how important it was to give my children the gift of time and to be fully present with them."

However, Pete's experience with his family was different than Abbey's. His dad was frequently absent and acted coldly toward him when he was at home. Pete experienced little affirmation or quality time with his dad, who was results driven. Pete also had to deal with his older brother being favored by his dad, due to an athletic prowess that Pete did not possess. Pete describes what it took for him and Abbey to become the parents they needed to be:

"We were fortunate to address our own sinful bents of selfishness and identify the failures of our parents in order to become who we truly wanted to be for our girls."

Pete was able to turn things around from his family of origin by learning how to play with the girls when he was at home. The girls know him as a playful dad who loves to sing, dance and goof around with them.

"I have learned how to be fully present when I am with the girls. I can give my best to the girls while at home and not feel guilty when I dedicate time to my career and future goals."

Abbey and Pete recognized their need to connect with God and become recipients of his grace, mercy and wisdom. They were able to avoid repeating some of the unhealthy parenting patterns from their families of origin as they allowed God to guide them through these struggles.

Parents who place children at the center of their lives will have many regrets because children will fail their expectations in many ways. Anything that replaces Jesus as the center of your life will fail you. However, parents will be prepared to become living sacrifices for their children if they embrace a Christian viewpoint: "It's about my need to grow in order to invite my children into what I have learned about God's love."

"Doing" and "Becoming"

Parenting Your Children into Adulthood has two tracks. The first track is about "doing." Parents "do" things to show nurture and love to their children. The "doing" part of parenting includes protecting, discipline, meeting physical and emotional needs, validating, educating and making disciples.

The second track is about "becoming." God wants to form parents' hearts to reflect his love, wisdom, justice and grace to their children, grandchildren and, hopefully, great-grandchildren.

Mike, a pastor, talks about his struggles with being a parent:

"Parenting has taught me how selfish I was. I had to make a choice. Would I be a cheerful dad who prioritized my children's need over my own or would I begrudgingly perform the duties of parenting and make everyone feel as if they were a burden to me? I was surprised that my life, marriage and family could be so enriched by me becoming a loving, playful and flexible husband and father."

Mike explains how he needed his wife, Helen, to help him get involved in the daily activities and needs of their children:

"There were many times when my commitment to be a playful and flexible dad was challenged by being mentally and physically exhausted from my workday. At these times, I had to seek another source of strength and compassion for my family. I found that God was more than able to give what I needed to be a faithful husband and father. My heart was now turned toward my family. I no longer saw them as a being in the way of performing my duties as a pastor. I gained a new perspective which I found very healing, as I realized how much God sacrificed for us as Father."

The "becoming" track is all about discovering God's heart for parents. In case you need to be reminded, God rejoices over you! Parents will learn more about God's love, grace, mercy and justice in their lives than in any other type of relationship, career or social interaction.

The Scriptures tell us that rarely will someone die for a righteous or good person (Romans 5:6–8). However, most parents would gladly give up their lives for their children. I would count it an honor to exchange my life for my child's due to sickness or an accident. However, I believe it is more noble and difficult to be a living sacrifice for your children than simply exchanging your death to extend their physical lives.

Sacrificial Love

Another way to describe the giving away of a parent's life is called sacrificial love. Sacrificial love is what God extends to us. He gave his only begotten Son to be the sacrificial Lamb that took away the sins of the world at the expense of his life (John 3:16). Children need the very life (love of God) within their parents in order to make healthy transitions from living lives based upon sustenance (life satisfied by the stomach or making life comfortable) to a life found only through a relationship with God (life that satisfies the soul).

Children desperately need parents who will love them sacrificially. Sacrificial love can be expressed through taking your children to tutors when necessary or attending their sporting events. The cost may be refusing overtime or spending days off with the children rather than on personal hobbies.

A fuller expression of sacrificial love is formed out of daily commitments to express godly love, such as extending peace, patience, mercy, kindness, goodness, honesty and gentleness to your children (Galatians 5:22–23). Children who receive these types of daily expressions of sacrificial love learn to return these characteristics to their parents later in life.

Children will experience successes and failures in their personal lives that require parents to demonstrate sacrificial love through mercy, forgiveness or encouragement. Our culture is desperate to see sacrificial love in action.

Jane, a single mom, describes how she was able to overcome the pain of growing up with a disconnected dad:

"My dad was absent most of the time. However, God began to reveal himself to me as a loving Father so that I could reveal his love to my children. I wanted to be a great mom, but I needed to experience a father's love. God is really there for me. He invests time in our relationship. He loves me and gives me wisdom that I am able to share with my children. I know there are times when I need to release control of my circumstances and trust God with my children. I have learned that I have a death grip of control whenever I do not trust God's love, mercy and provision for my family. Understanding God as my Father has reshaped my understanding of being a parent. He does not expect us to be perfect but faithful children (parents). God allows me to be a parent and he is equipping me to be the parent I want to be."

Parents who recognize these types of personal struggles to love their children sacrificially will discover that God will help them to overcome any obstacle, whether spiritual, relational or cultural, in order to form loving relationships with them. God redeems and restores what was missing in parents' lives due to unhealthy family systems as they were growing up. Parents who focus on preparing their children to become faithful and relationally healthy adults will be able to put their personal failures as well as the failures of their children in proper perspective. Failures and struggles do not define the value of someone's life. Always remember, God is a parent's best friend and advocate.

Fortunately, God understands parents' limited capacity to love their children sacrificially on a daily basis. He is able to refresh and renew parents' ability to love as they learn to pray and ask for strength, grace and patience from him. This is what it means to allow God to parent you as you parent your children.

Discussion Questions

1. What does sacrificial love look like between you and your children?
2. How did your parents model sacrificial love in your family of origin?

The Two Enemies of Sacrificial Love

Individualism and self-reliance are perhaps the two greatest threats to sacrificial love. Individualism seeks what is best for the individual rather than giving his or her best to the relationship. Self-reliance is a partner to individualism. Personal advancement and personal happiness are the goals of a self-reliant person.

Parents who are resistant to or unaware of God's love will default to individualism and self-reliance as their parenting styles. Children will become very anxious if they are put in situations or circumstances where their parent's happiness is dependent on their behaviors or compliance. Parents will experience great depths of joy and peace knowing that God is pleased with their efforts to love their children sacrificially. Happiness is knowing that God knows your heart and is pleased with you.

Our culture is suspicious of sacrificial love. For many people, sacrificial love evokes a sense of self-annihilation (Holeman, 2008). Self-annihilation is giving oneself over to another human being. In essence, your life, dreams or goals are secondary to that of the other person.

The love that I am describing between parent and child is far from the concept of self-annihilation. Sacrificial love and self-denial are types of love that come from giving ourselves over to God as Father and Lord. Anyone who gives their life to Christ will truly discover their purpose in life (John 15:5).

Each person was created to be an expression of love, grace, mercy and justice to the world. Parents who willingly and joyfully love their children at the cost of their own desires, comforts and personal development will find more strength, comfort and compassion flowing into their lives.

Parents who demonstrate sacrificial love to their children actually introduce them to their heavenly Father. Sacrificial love is a divine attribute that confirms the reality of something greater than humanity. Each recipient of sacrificial love is left with the question: "What is the source of this type of love?" Parents will have many opportunities to extend sacrificial love toward their children by introducing them to redemptive love. For many children, their journey of discovering God's irresistible love begins as a result of their parents' demonstration of sacrificial love to them.

Lisa, a mother of two, talks about her need to be creative in the way she expresses love to her children. She has a thirteen-year-old son and a nine-year-old daughter.

"One day I would somehow hit the target with both children, other days they would not be receptive to how I showed them affection twenty-four hours earlier. I learned how important it was to spend time with God and be in a loving relationship with him before I set

*out to be a parent for the day. My time with God became the cata-
lyst to loving my children. I was not focused on how the children
responded to me, but how I could love them. If they were unrespon-
sive to my loving acts or expressions, I did not take it as a personal
failure. I wanted to learn how to love them individually. No longer
was I expecting both of them to respond similarly to my expressions
of love. God gave me insight on how to love them uniquely, just like
he loves me. Some days it was hugs, other days not so much. But
just as God responds to us, we can learn to respond to our children.
I had to be creative in the way I was able to express love to my
daughter. I learned to tune into her, as God does with me, gently
and lovingly."*

Cultural vs. Christian Values

In my opinion, today's child-centered parenting strategies overem-
phasize the physical, social and educational needs of children at the
expense of spiritual and character development. I see many parents
wearing themselves out by focusing on these cultural values.

Parents must draw their strength, love, wisdom, truth and justice
from God's Word in order to balance cultural priorities that cannot
be avoided in this life. In many cases, these cultural priorities serve as
examples that parents can use to demonstrate the differences between
secular and Christian values.

Christian families are able to model Christlikeness to the parents
of their children's friends as they participate in athletics, dance or
academic advancement. Children, like parents, have been set apart
in order to influence their peers.

I am amazed at how adept our culture is at educating children
in the values of personal and social advancement. Children quickly
gain expectations of their parents to buy into these values and all that
comes with them. Parents must learn to balance these cultural values

by intentionally focusing on the character and spiritual development of their children. Children will benefit from participating in activities that increase physical and social development. However, these areas do not prepare children to be mature adults and future parents who will love their spouses and children sacrificially.

The Parenting Adult Children (PAC) Model

Children who receive the characteristics of sacrificial love, as experienced through nurture, values, mutuality and interdependence, will have a great start in becoming mature disciples and future spouses and parents. The PAC Model enables all parents including single, step, foster and adoptive parents to develop spiritual and practical strategies that meet the physical, emotional and spiritual needs of their children.

The Parenting Model protects against these types of outcomes that are common when children do not have a relational model to follow:

1. Children who do not receive the benefits of the *Nurture* stage will often look for future spouses who will either nurture them, almost like a parent and child relationship, or they will value independence rather than interdependence (disconnected).

2. Children who do not receive the benefits of the *Values* stage look for future spouses who allow them to make their own rules for life or they are attracted to someone who is very stable and responsible to make up for their inability to establish proper boundaries. Typically, when the latter occurs, only one person in the relationship is making all of the decisions. The spouse with strong values feels as if they are the only adult in the relationship.

3. Children who do not receive the benefits of the *Mutuality* stage look for future spouses who will not challenge them to be mutually respectful and responsible or they look for

someone who tells them what to do and how to do it.

4. Children who do not receive the benefits of the *Interdependence* stage look for future spouses who will not hold them accountable for their actions or they look for someone who plays the role of a police officer. The spouse who serves as a police officer becomes responsible to catch her/his husband or wife doing something wrong before they confess to any wrongful behaviors. Someone who does not learn to become interdependent often does not have the maturity to confess wrongdoing and self-correct unless he/she is caught in the act.

None of these possible outcomes fosters healthy marital relationships.

Parenting strategies need to reach beyond a child's eighteenth birthday. Unfortunately, I have seen many of the extreme examples mentioned above being lived out in premarital and marital relationships over the last ten years.

The characteristics of nurture, values, mutuality and interdependence are foundational principles of successful adulthood. These characteristics help children to avoid self-centered behavior that is damaging to their future marriage relationships. The family is a child's best hope to become a mature disciple and loving spouse.

Life in Motion Resources

In order to encourage growth and enrichment in marriages and families, Life in Motion Resources is offering our readers a free Parenting Inventory (LIMRI). You can find out more about the LIMRI at www.lifeinmotionresources.com. To receive the free inventory, go to www.limri.org/parent.

The LIMRI is an online assessment tool that churches, counselors and Christian organizations utilize to enrich relationships of members, clients, staff, leadership or employees. Couples answer demographic questions that generate statements unique to dating, engaged or married couples. The common targets include: communication, conflict resolution, spiritual life, shared spiritual life, financial, personality, respect, emotional honesty, and relationship satisfaction. Dating, engaged or married couples with children also receive Parenting and Parenting Our Children Targets. Couples with children from former relationships receive: Parenting His or Her Children Targets. The Future Sexual Relationship Target is exclusive to engaged couples. Married couples receive the Sexual Relationship Target.

The LIMRI is a reliable and valid instrument that measures friendship and shared values. These characteristics have a unique relationship with couple satisfaction. Scoring fifty-five percent or above in friendship and sixty-four percent in shared values equal couple satisfaction. The LIMRI generates worksheets and growth plans that allow couples to grow friendship and shared values that sustain and grow couple satisfaction in dating, engaged and marriage relationships. I serve as the President of Life in Motion Resources.

In the following chapters, you will learn more about the LIMRI and worksheets.

CHAPTER TWO

Nurture

Nurture	**Values**	**Mutuality**	**Interdependence**
0–6 years	7–12 years	13–18 years	19–27 years

The Nurture stage lays the foundation of trust and sacrificial love between parents and children. Parents express nurture to their children in many ways, including feeding, bathing, changing diapers, holding, comforting, encouraging, praying and playing. Parents who willingly meet these physical and emotional needs experience great satisfaction as peace and calm come over their children from these expressions of nurture.

However, there comes a time in every infant's life when milk only satisfies their bellies or a fresh diaper only meets an immediate need for cleanliness and comfort. The basic needs of children quickly move beyond their need for a meal or a clean diaper. Children begin to need more of their parents' hearts or character than life-giving sustenance.

Transition – From Trust to Character Development

Most parents anticipate meeting the physical needs of their children: milk, food, clothing and shelter. These things are critical and practical elements of nurturing children. However, the greater challenge lies ahead when children need different types of nurture. Items such as food, clothing and shelter sustain life, but character is life-giving. Children need to feed off of the very character of their parents, starting between four and six years of age.

The character of the parent becomes more important to a child than all other types of nurture. Godly character is what satisfies the deepest needs of a child's soul. Parents develop life-giving character as they allow God to parent them.

Melissa, a missionary, writes:

"There was a huge amount of nurture involved in how God helped us to overcome our self-doubt in regards to an overseas mission appointment. We had fears over how we would provide for our kids. We have five young children, who would be susceptible to

viruses, parasites, impure water sources, to name only of a few of the safety concerns of moving to another country. It was overwhelming to consider all of the medical and safety concerns of our children. We questioned ourselves whether we should expose our children to these types of environments. Another concern was over our finances. Where was the money going to come from? Our story is all about God's faithfulness. Our children were able to experience firsthand how God provides and protects us. We could only consider such things because God spoke to our hearts. We felt God was asking us, 'How much do you love your children?' God replied, 'I love them more!' We came to learn that God is wild and passionately crazy about our kids, even more so than we are. This is so hard to imagine, but we came to realize how true it was."

Parents must successfully navigate between meeting the physical needs of their children and providing life-giving sustenance. Melissa had to trust God with the health and welfare of their children.

Melissa's children will forever be changed by the willingness of their parents to put their lives in God's hands to serve as missionaries. Life is all about learning to live on God's terms, not on your terms. Living for yourself and personal advancement is what secular cultures invite you to embrace.

Parents who fail to recognize the transitions needed for their children to move beyond sustenance to character development may find themselves facing a crisis in their own lives. Parents can feel as if they give and give to their children, even at the expense of their personal needs, desires, responsibilities and goals. Some parents lose a sense of their personal identities meeting all of their children's needs.

Children will always want more of what their parents have to offer as they teach them to become people of faith, integrity, honesty and justice. Parents will find themselves in an amazing paradigm as children want more of their hearts while time and availability are limited. The church is an excellent resource for parents. Churches partner with parents as they disciple their children.

Children in this stage are learning how to form trusting relationships with their parents. Parents hold the answers to eternal life as well as the physical and emotional needs of their children. Children ask their parents questions that would not be directed toward anyone else because they trust them. Nothing satisfies children's souls like asking questions of their parents.

Children quickly transition away from their primary need for sustenance to character development. The question-asking phase is a good indicator of this transitional phase.

Technology

At times, parents struggle with this transitional stage because they are too busy to answer every why and how question being asked by their children. Too often, parents substitute electronic stimulation (media) for personal interaction with their children through video games and DVDs. In essence, parents use technology/electronics to distract their children from a very taxing but necessary stage of developmental needs.

I am concerned how technology limits opportunities for parents to transfer godly character and model trust and trustworthiness to their children. In my experience, children will quickly learn that their parents are too busy to connect with them, while technology never rejects them. I have seen children become irritated with their parents at restaurants and the only way to redirect them is to turn on some type of technology.

Technology is not an enemy of parenting. In many ways technology enriches children's learning potential. But technology cannot foster happiness, maturity or identity in their lives. These things require lots of interactions with moms and dads. These interactions between parents and children are sacred. Technology, when used incorrectly, creates a false sense of intimacy and nurturing between parents and children.

I am the first person to acknowledge that parents need time and space, not only to get things done, but also to invest in their own spiritual and emotional health. The following suggestions are intended to help parents be creative in their use of technology. This can help them to avoid overuse due to poor planning or responding to unexpected interruptions in their day.

- Carry educational games in your car, such as flash cards (animals, shapes, and numbers) and books. Parents can find hundreds of ideas by searching the web for hands-on children's educational games.

- Limit TV or media viewing to two hours per night.

- Download stories or books to your electronic devices that will encourage your children to read rather than watch a cartoon or video.

- Download educational videos about animals and habitat rather than cartoons or movies.

- No TV in children's bedrooms.

Parents will find that God is willing and able to fill them with love, mercy and truth whenever they turn toward him for help. They can trust God to fill them with these attributes because he is a faithful Father. In the same way children learn to turn to their parents when they have needs that cannot be filled by anyone else. Parental failures or struggles should drive moms and dads toward their heavenly Father for help and encouragement.

Discussion Questions

1. What are the most pressing issues/needs that you face as a parent?
2. Which of these characteristics do you struggle with the most? Honesty, integrity, purity, fear, control, trust, etc.

3. Do your children struggle with integrity, purity, honesty, fear, or control?

Sacred Shelters

Delores Leckey describes Christian homes as sacred shelters where family members experience acceptance and nurture (Thompson, 1998). Sacred shelters do not create isolated environments where people are hidden away from the pain, brokenness or influence of the world. Families can overcome the brokenness of the world by making their homes sacred shelters.

All family members struggle with their sinful natures. At times everyone tends to be self-centered and controlling. Family is the place where parents and siblings acknowledge their personal struggles and learn to express love and forgiveness toward one another for failing to live out integrity and honesty on a daily basis.

Family provides frameworks for faith, healing and solace from a chaotic and abusive world. Christian families have been reconciled to God and have the best opportunity to demonstrate reconciliation of struggling or broken relationships. Family is all about discovering your spiritual identity, unconditional love, and empowerment to fulfill God's purposes individually and corporately (Thompson, 1998).

The PAC Model will help you to establish your home as a sacred shelter.

Negative vs. Positive Parenting Traits

The table below compares negative and positive parental responses in the Nurture stage (0–6 years). Parents need to address difficult circumstances in positive ways to avoid shame, guilt or fear from becoming embedded in their children's lives.

Negative parenting traits	Positive parenting traits
Shame-based parenting style (Erikson)	It's normal for children to explore their bodies or act inappropriately at times.
Guilt-based parenting style	Parents should not overreact when children say "no" to them because this is a pathway of learning autonomy (Erikson).
Fear-based parenting style	Children need to be instructed about being cautious around strangers without becoming fearful of people they do not know.
Overly cautious parenting style (safety oriented)	Parents need to be careful about expressing too much concern over children getting hurt playing sports, being outside without a coat, etc.
Permissive parenting style (unable to tell children "No.")	Parents need to develop healthy boundaries that teach children critical thinking skills. Children need to learn how to avoid unsafe environments, such as playing in the street, handling knives, tools, etc.

Unhealthy vs. Healthy Characteristics of Nurture

The table below compares unhealthy vs. healthy characteristics of nurture. The healthy characteristics will guide parents in repairing areas of broken trust with their children. Children will be blessed as parent's model the healthy characteristics of nurture. It is never too late to model any of the healthy characteristics of nurture to your children.

Unhealthy characteristics of nurture	Healthy characteristics of nurture
Parents using their children as confidants for their needs and concerns.	Listening without judging as their children express their needs or ideas.
Expecting children to provide emotional support to parents.	Providing support, encouragement and affirmation.

Insisting that children spend time with parents (because it is what they need).	Creating opportunities for quality time with their children.
Requiring children to hug or kiss them even when their children do not want to be affectionate at that moment.	Providing children with appropriate physical affection.

Exercise

- Identify the healthy characteristics of nurture that you regularly express to your children.

- Identify any of the unhealthy characteristics that you may express to your children.

- What is motivating you to express any of these unhealthy characteristics toward your children?

- How can you be more intentional about creating a nurturing environment in your home?

- See the Appendix for a sample Parent Plan.

Discussion Questions

1. How does God reveal his presence to you and your family? Think back and recall examples when God's love was poured out to you or your children.
2. Take time to reflect on God's faithfulness to you and your children. What form has this taken in your life?
3. How can you involve your children in remembering God's faithfulness to your family?

Nurturing Relationships

One of the most challenging aspects of parenting is learning to develop nurturing relationships with your children throughout each stage of the Parenting Model (Nurture, Values, Mutuality and Interdependence). Nurture is just as important to other age groups in the PAC Model as it is in the Nurture stage (0–6 years old).

The way parents express nurture in each age group needs to be creative and flexible, because each child is different in regard to receiving and expressing nurture. Fortunately, parents can discover the nurturing bents of their children by watching how they respond to other adults or children. Parents will find suggestions on how to express nurture to children in each stage of the PAC Model.

Parenting Resources

The PAC Model is supported by the research collected from the Life in Motion Relationships Inventory. The LIMRI measures areas of nurture, values, mutuality and interdependence in family relationships. The LIMRI is a values-based inventory identifying strengths and areas of improvement needed in parent-to-parent, child-to-parent and sibling relationships.

- The Parenting Target identifies strengths and areas of improvement needed in couples as they co-parent their children.

- The Parenting Our Children Target identifies strengths and areas of improvement needed between children and parents.

- The Parenting His Children Target identifies strengths and areas of improvement needed between the man and his children, and the relationship between his children and his wife (stepparent).

- The Parenting Her Children Target identifies strengths and areas of improvement needed between the woman and her children and the relationship between her children and her husband (stepparent).

In order to support and encourage parents, Life in Motion Resources has developed worksheets and growth plans that utilize Scriptures, Principles, Discussion Questions and Practical Applications to give couples spiritual and practical insights to discuss and implement into their family life.

The LIMRI helps couples to identify and celebrate their strengths in parenting and family life. Growth plans and worksheets allow couples to gain new insights and skills in areas where improvement is needed in parent-to-parent, child-to-parent and sibling relationships.

Parents reporting couple satisfaction agree on the factors listed below (Hitchcock, 2013):

Self-view	Other's view (Spouse)
I often ask my spouse for his/her opinion.	My spouse often asks me for my opinion.
I am supportive of my spouse's parenting values (i.e. honesty, integrity and faith).	My spouse is supportive of my parenting values (honesty, integrity and faith).
I show affection to the children.	My spouse shows affection to the children.
I spend an appropriate amount of quality time with our children.	My spouse spends an appropriate amount of quality time with our children.
Our children respond well to my affection and initiative toward them.	Our children respond well to my spouse's affection and initiative toward them.
I am receptive to our children's affection.	My spouse is receptive to our children's affection.
Our children show respect to me.	Our children show respect toward my spouse.

Place a plus sign (+) next to the statements in the Self-view column in the table above that describe behaviors that you display frequently and place a minus sign (-) next to the statements that you display less frequently. Use the same symbols to assess your spouse, fiancé or boy/girlfriend's frequency or infrequency in the Other's view column.

The worksheets are modeled after an ancient Christian discipline of *Lectio Divina*. This traditional Benedictine practice of Scripture reading, meditation and prayer is intended to promote communion with God and to increase the knowledge of God's Word. It does not treat Scripture as texts to be studied, but as the Living Word (Wikipedia, 2015).

Couples meditate on the Scriptures, Principles, Discussion Questions and Practical Applications before answering the questions in each section of the worksheets. The man and woman complete the first half of the worksheet individually and then share their answers with each other. Spiritual conversations happen naturally as the couple share insights from their worksheets in response to the Scriptures, Principles, Discussion Questions and Practical Applications.

Couples also receive insight on how to pray for each other as they discuss key words or principles that were significant to them. One spouse may say: "I was impressed with the idea of being watchful and devoted in our prayer life. I believe the Lord is showing me that I need to be attentive to this area of our relationship." His or her spouse will then know how to pray for them: "Lord, help my husband/wife to be diligent in being watchful and devoted to his/her prayer life."

The man and woman are given separate four-digit pin numbers to ensure privacy. Neither the man nor the woman can see the other's answers or dialogue with their coaches as they complete the first half of the worksheet. The top section of each worksheet offers spiritual and practical insights that couples use to strengthen and enrich areas of their relationships and parenting responsibilities.

The second half of the worksheet is the Couple's Worksheet Section. This section is completed by couples working together. Couples can log in as either the man or woman in order to complete this.

See the following Sample Worksheets:

Strength Worksheet

Worksheet – Nurturing Home Agreement – Strength

Statement: Our home is a nurturing environment for our children.

- Wife agrees with: "Our home is a nurturing environment for our children."

- Husband agrees with: "Our home is a nurturing environment for our children."

Scripture

Please meditate on the Scripture below for two days, then answer the following questions.

Deuteronomy 6:6–9: "These commandments that I give you today are to be upon your hearts. Impress them on your children. Talk about them when you sit at home and when you walk along the road, when you lie down and when you get up. Tie them as symbols on your hands and bind them on your foreheads. Write them on the doorframes of your houses and on your gates."

Participants: Husband & Wife

What key words or phrases in this Scripture are relevant to you and your relationship with your spouse and your children?

Participants: Husband & Wife

How can this Scripture apply to the statement: "Our home is a nurturing environment for our children"?

Principles

1. Your home must be the safest environment your children will experience throughout their childhood.
2. A home needs to have a balance between mercy and discipline.
3. A home must be a safe place for children to fail and then experience forgiveness.
4. A home is a place to overcome negative bents and develop biblical values and Christian character.

Participants: Husband & Wife

Select the principle that is most relevant to you.

Participants: Husband & Wife

How does this principle apply to your life and relationship with your spouse?

Couple's Worksheet Section (to be completed together)

Husband's Strength Questions

Husband asks Wife: "How do I contribute in making our home a nurturing place for our children?"

Give one or two examples.

Wife's Strength Questions

Wife asks Husband: "How do I contribute in making our home a nurturing place for our children?"

Give one or two examples.

Improvement Needed Worksheet

Worksheet – Parenting Brings Us Closer
Disagreement – Improvement Needed

Statement: Parenting has brought us closer in our marriage.

- Wife disagrees with: "Parenting has brought us closer in our marriage."
- Husband agrees with: "Parenting has brought us closer in our marriage."

Scripture

Please meditate on the Scripture below for two days then answer the following questions.

Psalms 78:3–7 ESV: "things that we have heard and known, that our fathers have told us. We will not hide them from their children, but tell to the coming generation the glorious deeds of the LORD, and his might, and the wonders that he has done. He established a testimony in Jacob and appointed a law in Israel, which he commanded our fathers to teach to their children, that the next generation might know them, the children yet unborn, and arise and tell them to their children, so that they should set their hope in God and not forget the works of God but keep his commandments."

Participants: Husband & Wife

What key words or phrases in this Scripture are relevant to you and your relationship with your spouse?

Participants: Husband & Wife

How can this Scripture apply to the statement: "Parenting has brought us closer in our marriage"?

Principles

1. Children are to be received as blessings from the Lord.
2. Parenting allows a couple to share in the formation of their children's identities.
3. Couples who work together to make their home a place of worship for their children will experience a home filled with God's presence.
4. Parents have an opportunity to establish a legacy of faith, love and servanthood in their family.
5. Parenting children requires parents to work as teammate's at the most important job in the world.

Participants: Husband & Wife

Select the principle that is most relevant to you.

Participants: Husband & Wife

How does this principle apply to your life and relationship with your spouse?

Discussion Questions

1. Do you regularly point out to your spouse how his/her spiritual gifts bless your children?
2. Do you and your spouse complement each other in the way that you parent your children?

Participants: Husband & Wife

Select the discussion question that was most relevant to you.

Participants: Husband & Wife

How does this discussion question apply to your life and relationship with your spouse?

Practical Application

Excerpt from *Parenting Your Children into Adulthood* by Ron Hitchcock The following information will help parents prepare their children to establish healthy relationships as adults.

Nurture stage (0–6 years) – Children are completely dependent upon their parents. Children at this stage are learning to form trusting relationships that will enrich all future relationships. The building blocks of trust are formed as parents meet the physical and emotional needs of their children.

Values stage (7–12 years) – Children learn to make decisions based upon the parents' values, such as honesty, respect, faith, responsibility and trust. Children in this age group are learning how to emulate these values (respect and responsibility) in their family relationships.

Mutuality stage (13–18 years) – During these years, most teens begin to push toward independence rather than interdependence. Parents that model mutuality will help their teens to be involved in interdependent relationships with them. Western culture promotes independence rather than interdependence making this process more difficult.

Interdependence stage (19–27 years) – Parents who respond to their adult children's choices or decisions without judgment will form friendships with them. Adult children who value interdependence are prepared to form premarital relationships that avoid the extremes of independence or enmeshment.

List a few of your husband's godly characteristics.

List a few of your wife's godly characteristics.

* Identify ways that your spouse's godly characteristics complement yours in parenting your children.
* Identify ways that make your home a place of worship.
* Identify ways to model servanthood to your children.
* Identify ways you are establishing a spirit of love in your home.

Couple's Worksheet Section (to be completed together)

Husband's Improvement Questions

Participants: Wife, Husband, Coach

Husband asks Wife: "In what ways can parenting create more closeness in our relationship?"

Husband asks Wife: "How can we be more intentional about working as a team in parenting?"

How can these changes enhance your relationship?

Wife's Improvement Questions

Participants: Wife, Husband, Coach

Wife asks Husband: "In what ways can parenting create more closeness in our relationship?"

Wife asks Husband: "How can we be more intentional about working as a team in our parenting?"

How can these changes enhance your relationship?

CHAPTER THREE

Values

Nurture	Values	Mutuality	Interdependence
0–6 years	7–12 years	13–18 years	19–27 years

The Golden Years

This stage helps develop values that influence the way family members respond to one another: parent to parent, parent to child and sibling to sibling.

The seven to twelve year age group is commonly known as the "Golden Years" of parenting. Parents with children in this stage have more influence than teachers, athletes or childhood friends. Children desire to spend more time with mom and dad than with anyone else. In this stage, most parent and child relationships have their highest levels of trust.

Parents can take advantage of these Golden Years by developing a value system that includes faith, respect, responsibility, communication, commitment, integrity, purity, truth, gratitude, honesty and conflict resolution. These values establish a template of how family members can relate to each other for the rest of their lives.

Discipline vs. Development of Values

Some parents with children in this stage inadvertently prioritize discipline over the development of values. Biblical values open a child's heart to discipline in a way that helps to form their character. Discipline without clear values often establishes power and control between parent and child rather than righteousness and justice. Parents who learn to associate discipline with values have begun the journey of empowering their children to be respectful, responsible and committed to each other. Children who reject the discipline of their parents will have the potential to develop attitudes of entitlement or intolerance toward others.

Children who refuse to pick up after themselves after being asked will deservedly experience some type of discipline such as time outs or loss of privileges. Children need to understand which value was tied to the disciplinary action. The parent needs to say: "You are being disciplined because you were disrespectful or irresponsible. Not only were you unwilling to pick up after yourself, but someone else had to carry the weight of your responsibility." The child will resist disciplinary actions that are not associated with a value system.

As children become older, they may rationalize their behavior by comparing their choices to others who are rebellious: "I don't do bad things like so many of my friends. Why should I be punished for not cleaning my room?" Children who use this type of defense do not understand the value behind disciplinary actions.

Children may never consider the value of cleaning up their bedrooms or washing the dishes as an important part of their character development. However, these are essential characteristics of a mature adult.

Responding Appropriately

Michelle writes:

"One of my biggest struggles was helping my children learn how to be responsible. I finally realized that my desire to control things and outcomes was the biggest enemy that prevented me from teaching the children to learn the value of responsibility. I liked having things done my way and to my standards. Since I could do a better job than my children were capable of doing, I justified my behavior. The result of my behavior kept my children from learning how to deal with failure in a healthy way. I did not want my children to fail at cleaning their room or by getting a poor grade on a homework assignment. I did not want my children to experience failure, so I made sure they did not have a chance to fail. It did not take long to figure out that I learned this trait from my parents. I wish that I had made room for them to fail a little, at least in the little things. It sounds funny to say, but I just wanted them to always succeed. I now understand that my parents did this for me as well.

They meant well, but letting me fail in some things would have been a good lesson for me.

"I realized that my parenting style was greatly affected when my husband left me and the children. I was grieving the loss of my marriage and I was so concerned for the loss that my children were experiencing. I wanted to make everything okay for my children. I feel I must warn people against trying to insulate children from loss and pain following a divorce. I cannot make everything right, only God can fill these empty places. My children felt more useful and secure after I gave them some ownership. We have become a team in the game of life. Children need to know that life will be different after Dad left, but we can still move on, even though we do not like the way life is now. We must accept these changes and go on with our lives. God has our backs and he has a bright future for our family."

Parents will benefit from taking time before responding to their children's personal struggles in order to avoid responding in fear, shame, guilt or anger. Many parents have personal bents toward high standards. Parents want their children to benefit from standards of excellence such as stability, integrity and honesty. These characteristics take time and encouragement, especially when children fail to meet these standards. Parents need to be slow in pointing out their children's faults or failures to live up to these values in order to avoid guilt, shame or fear of failure from gaining a foothold in their lives. However, parents need to act quickly to stop behaviors that have harmful or long-term consequences, such as drug or alcohol abuse, or abusive peer or dating relationships.

Fortunately, most of the struggles in children's character or behaviors will not need to have immediate or strong responses. Parents are highly motivated to help their children avoid consequences due to sinful or ignorant behavior. But remember that children must learn how to overcome choices or negative attitudes by experiencing natural consequences. Parents who lose sight of God's patience, mercy and grace can put themselves in the position of being their children's judge. They may try to uproot or purge unhealthy behaviors out of their children's hearts rather than teaching them how to take their failures to God and seek forgiveness and mercy.

I was impressed with the following quote, unfortunately I could not find its origin: "My sin does not look good on anyone else." I would add: "Especially on my child." Parents can easily justify their own personal struggles and sinful bents, but respond too quickly or harshly when they see these same things in their children's behavior or attitudes.

Child Focused vs. God Centered

God understands the demands that children bring into parents' lives. He is able to fill parents with his love, grace, wisdom and patience in order to meet their children's needs. Some of these needs include poor health, learning disabilities, poor social skills and behavioral struggles that cannot be changed by the parent, no matter how hard they try.

In order to help, sociologists have identified developmental stages, including the educational, social, emotional and physical needs of children. The science behind many parenting books helps moms and dads to parent their children from a developmental process.

I believe these books have created a child-focused parenting culture that places the attention on child development rather than on parental development. A child-focused culture has the potential to put children rather than God at the center of parents' lives. Parents who keep God at the center of their lives will be able to incorporate the information from these developmental studies to enrich their parenting styles. A Christ-centered parenting model enriches the lives of parents, enabling them to raise their children from a biblical rather than a cultural perspective.

Jim, a dad to three boys, writes:

"My greatest need is honesty and integrity as a man and father. The Bible instructs us to come boldly before the throne of God. I understand this to mean that I am able to come before God with any problem or negative circumstance that is a result of my struggle with honesty and integrity. It does not matter how trivial or traumatic these problems seem compared to everything else that is going on in the world. God has promised that he is able to give me a peace that passes all understanding (John 14:27).

"There are times when I feel powerless to change things in my children's lives that have the potential to create attitudes of entitlement or self-centeredness. I would like to be able to insulate them from the cultural values that are contrary to a biblical worldview that is based upon loving others and being content with what you have. However, I am learning that when I am struggling with honesty and integrity or when I feel that I am failing as a parent, that I can cast all my cares upon him because he cares for me (1 Peter 5:7). All of this means that God loves me and will help me to overcome my personal struggles so that I can pass on to my children the hope that God is a loving Father who cares for us as a family.

"When I parent out of fear or dishonesty, I can never be truthful with myself or my children. I have tried to let my children know that God knows and sees everything. He sees our strengths and our warts. I tell them that God is not looking for perfection from us. He simply desires that we believe in his Son and willingly follow him. I try to let my children know I am not here to punish them but rather to guide them as God guides me. My honesty and transparency with my children is a reflection of Gods openness in dealing with me and working out his plan in my life."

Authentic Faith

The end result of parenthood leads to the discovery of God as their Father. As with all journeys, there are times of excitement and times of trepidation. The parent who stays committed to the journey will discover a richness of God's presence that cannot be found in other ways.

Sometimes parents can be overly concerned about their child's response to faith. Parents can make the mistake of seeing every action or behavior of their child as either an expression or a rejection of faith. When this happens, parents can become heavy-handed in their approach to discipline in order to turn children away from behaviors that are interpreted as statements against faith.

Cheryl, a single mom, shares her struggle to establish the value of faith in her home:

> *"I wanted my children to grow up with a strong faith that would guide them through any trial that could come their way. My method of teaching was to model my faith to my children. I began to struggle to be a good example because, at times, my faith was weak. I would become discouraged when things were not working the way I had planned. Too often, I found myself struggling to do the right thing in response to my personal trials. I had to learn how to be honest about my personal struggles in order to model an authentic faith to my children."*

Cheryl learned a valuable lesson about being authentic with her faith. Parents who withhold their personal struggles from their children are not directing them to take these types of behavior or attitudes to the Lord. However, it is important to discuss only personal struggles that are age appropriate with your children. Cheryl wanted her children to know that they can take fear, anger, doubt or moral and ethical failures to God, who loves, forgives and empowers them to overcome these faults.

Discussion Questions

1. How does Jim's struggle with honesty and integrity impact his parenting style?
2. How does your personal struggle with integrity, honesty, purity, etc. affect your marriage and parenting style?
3. Do you feel that mercy and grace are prominent characteristics in your home?
4. How would your family benefit from making your home a sacred shelter?
5. What can you do to start the process of making your home a sacred shelter?

Establishing Positive Values

The following table will help parents to establish values that will turn children away from negative behaviors or attitudes:

Behaviors that require disciplinary actions	Values that guide your discipline
Talking back or yelling	**Respectful communication:** Children can disagree, but they must be respectful.
Hitting siblings	**Safety:** No one has a right to harm others. You must learn to express anger in healthy ways.
Expressing entitlement or being dismissive toward parental authority	**Gratitude:** Children who learn to express gratitude will learn that all good things are a gift. Entitlement leads to children feeling that they are owed or own things. _Thankfulness_ is expressing appreciation for something received. _Gratitude_ happens when children recognize that anything that is good is from God and their parents.

Breaking objects that do not belong to them	**Respect and conflict resolution:** Children who break objects often feel that there is no way to resolve conflicts, express their dissatisfaction with their parents' decisions or respond to disciplinary actions they interpret as unjust.
Unfinished homework assignments	**Responsibility and honesty:** Children who do not complete or falsify their homework assignments may feel that they cannot measure up to other students or their parents' expectations. Children may feel embarrassed about needing to work harder to complete assignments that other students complete quickly. They may also need help with time management.
Lying	**Truth:** Children who tell lies are often trying to escape undesirable consequences for their behavior. It is important to identify any patterns of lying, such as taking/stealing things. Some children take things to feel equal to others or as an act of justice when they do not have the same possessions or privileges as their friends or siblings.
Telling stories	**Integrity:** Children who tell stories or make wild exaggerations are often unsure of their value in the eyes of other people. Storytelling is not primarily a way to avoid discipline or consequences for poor decisions. Children need to be noticed by someone they care about or they are trying to capture someone's attention. Parents need to increase the amount of time and attention they are currently giving a child who has developed patterns of storytelling.

Boundaries

Boundaries teach children how to respect people, property and personal space. At first, boundaries may seem to create distance between people. However, boundaries have the opposite effect on relationships and family life. Boundaries are needed when someone is unable to validate or respect another person's personal space, possessions, beliefs or opinions. Boundaries are meant to be short-term interventions that serve as catalysts for change between two or more people.

Biblical values of marriage and family life will naturally form relational boundaries between couples, parents, siblings and extended family members. The Bible teaches that respect, humility, servanthood, generosity, thanksgiving, and submission as nonnegotiable attitudes and behaviors between brothers and sisters in Christ. These values form a Christian worldview that life is not exclusively about you. Children will learn how to establish respectful relationships from these types of values.

The Values stage of the PAC Model prepares children in the seven to twelve age group to overcome selfish behaviors and attitudes of entitlement that are common among teens and young adults. Many teens and young adults are influenced to embrace cultural norms that are often contrary to biblical values. Children who learn to practice and honor boundaries between parents and siblings will be prepared to form healthy relational boundaries with peers and in personal relationships for the rest of their lives.

The goals of boundaries need to be clearly defined in order for each person to understand their value in relationships. For example, we agree to practice active listening by allowing each person to finish speaking before responding to what was said. Active listening is repeating back what the other person said: "I heard you say …" Whenever someone violates these agreements, it is necessary to restate the boundary and its goals. However, once the person honors the boundary, it does not have to be discussed again unless it is broken.

Boundaries create respectful rhythms between couples, allowing them to relate appropriately to each other. In new relationships boundaries may seem unnecessary but couples will quickly learn that respect, humility, servanthood and deference are core values that do not appear by chance. Boundaries protect relationships from abusive behaviors.

Most boundaries will serve as catalysts for change over short periods of time.

The table below identifies healthy boundaries in family relationships. The boundaries between parents and children will serve as the foundation for healthy boundaries between siblings.

Boundaries between parent and child	Boundaries between siblings
Parents ask rather than demand that their children talk about their emotions, bodies, fears and spiritual life.	Children learn to develop and respect personal boundaries by watching their parents interact with each other. Siblings will learn to respect each other's emotions, bodies, and faith by modeling respectful attitudes that parents show to other siblings.
Parents knock on their child's bedroom door before entering the room.	Siblings will learn to respect each other's private space and possessions by emulating their parents' respect for privacy or personal space.

Teens and young adults must be able to develop emotional, physical and spiritual boundaries in their friendships and dating relationships. At times, children will question the relevance of boundaries that parents feel are non-negotiable values of family life. Parents need to remember that children are influenced by cultural values that challenge the biblical values of love, respect, responsibility, faith and submission. This is why parents are so important in children's lives. Children will eventually learn that the world does not love them or have their best interest in mind. Parents must be committed to helping their children overcome behaviors that can impede their ability to become healthy adults, loving spouses or parents one day.

The Golden Rule vs. the Law

The primary rule (boundary) in every home should reflect the "Golden Rule": treat others the way you want to be treated (Matthew 7:12). Children will struggle with the Golden Rule because they must learn the discipline of delayed gratification. Parents must remember that delayed gratification is an essential characteristic for children to become mature adults. Most children will find it difficult to wait, work and strive for something that they desire right now.

Parents establish rules to guide their children into maturity. However, there should only be a few rules, and all of them need to be reasonable, measurable and repeatable. Good rules will add value to children's character as they develop respect, delayed gratification and faith. The following table (Hitchcock, 2013) will help parents to establish rules that are prescriptive (orthodox) rather than proscriptive (banning):

Bad Rules	Good Rules
Don't talk back.	When you disagree, show respect in what you say.
If you don't have anything nice to say, don't say anything at all.	Be truthful and loving when you are expressing your feelings. (Critique, but do not be critical.)
Never leave your dishes in the family room.	Respect others by cleaning up after yourself.
Don't rock the boat.	Challenge the opinions of others by asking why they believe the way they do about a subject and share why you believe the way you do.
Don't let people know when you are confused or hurting emotionally.	Confide in someone you trust with things that are troubling you.

Don't get emotional.	Respect others' emotions by allowing them to feel differently than you about things.
Don't cry.	Be sensitive when others cry – they care deeply about what is going on.
If you don't give it your best, don't even try.	Allow your children to fail. It is important that parents do not take the failure of their children personally. Failure can be an important character-building experience for children.
Don't think about yourself.	You can think about yourself, but do not be selfish, especially when things do not go your way.

The majority of emotional and physical struggles that children need to overcome represents generational coding that is unique to each family. Children are born into families that have histories of alcoholism, anxiety and anger or allergies and learning disabilities. Parents must identify these specific or unique needs in order to help them to overcome behaviors that are rooted in anger, guilt, fear or shame. Some of these behaviors surface as children struggle with learning or physical disabilities, chaotic homes, or insufficient financial resources.

Positive Parenting vs. Negative Parenting

The following table contrasts positive and negative parenting outcomes. Parents who practice these positive parenting responses will create homes that are sacred shelters.

Opportunities to meet unique needs in children	Discounting children's unique needs in order to toughen them up
Working with children to move from dependence to interdependence at a pace that is comfortable for them.	Requiring "separation" without considering children's ages, temperaments or readiness/maturity.

Helping children by teaching life skills.	Unwillingness to help children accomplish tasks or skills that they are unable to manage on their own.
Encouraging your children to share their concerns and seek advice.	Discouraging children from expressing their "needs" or for time alone with parents.
Offering empathy and encouragement when your child is uncertain, struggling with relationships or failing to succeed in academics, athletics or extracurricular activities.	Shaming a child for being afraid, uncertain or failing to live up to the expectations of others.

Compliant Children

The goal of the Values stage is to prepare children to transition into the next stage – mutuality between parents and teens. These rules or family values will expose your children's struggle with their sinful bents.

The Bible describes the importance of the Law for both Jews and Gentiles. The Law, also known as the Ten Commandments, allows each person to identify unhealthy behaviors or underdeveloped character traits (Romans 5–7). Without the Law, people would be unable to recognize ungodly behaviors and attitudes.

It is essential for parents to understand that ungodly behaviors can be masked by a child's compliance to the rules. Compliant children need just as much redirection (parenting) as strong-willed children. Despite appearances, a compliant child's heart may be far from repentance over negative attitudes or behaviors. This pattern is revealed in the story of the Prodigal Son's older brother (Luke 15). The jealousy of the older brother was triggered when his father threw a celebration for his rebellious younger son.

Parents need godly wisdom to recognize unhealthy behaviors that children struggle with internally. Parents who talk about their own struggles with unhealthy behaviors like jealousy, anger or judgment invite their children to self-report their own struggles. This normalizes their struggles with a broken humanity. Most likely jealousy was always a struggle for the older son, but it may have remained hidden until the younger son was celebrated. Jealousy surfaces when someone feels as if they deserve something due to their good behavior or faithfulness to meet all of the rules.

The older son wanted to be celebrated for all the wrong reasons. People can be rule followers, but their hearts are full of judgment or jealousy toward others. The father had established a safe and prosperous lifestyle for both of his children. The older brother became jealous when his younger brother was forgiven for his self-indulgent lifestyle.

Someone's adherence to biblical Law does not make him or her righteous or mature. Rule following can point the way to maturity and holiness but righteousness and holiness are found only in a personal relationship with Jesus.

Differentiation

"Differentiation" describes a child's ability to separate his or her own intellectual and emotional functioning from that of their parents (Wikipedia, 2015). Children who are taught differentiation form unique identities that are able to stand against peer pressure and cultural values. A differentiated person is able to hold onto a non-anxious presence when others around them are in crisis or chaotic environments (Friedman, 1985). Differentiation on a relational level can be described as:

1. Maintaining your integrity and well-being without intruding on that of others; and

2. Defining yourself and staying in touch with others. Differentiation allows people to be relational in anxious systems, relationships, or family life. Non-differentiated people tend to

cut others off when someone does not validate their feelings or emotions.

Another way to describe differentiation is having an "I" (identity = self-differentiated) and entering into a relationship with another "I" (identity = self-differentiated) without losing yourself or diminishing the self (identity) of the other (Stienke, 2006).

The parent and child relationship has the potential to establish the benefits of differentiation for all future relationships in a child's life. Children will benefit most from the benefits of differentiation during the Mutuality stage (13–18 years). Differentiation can help children in this age group avoid becoming competitive with their siblings or emulating rebellious or fearful behaviors that are common among their peers.

Teens who do not have the benefits of differentiation being modeled in their homes are more likely to fit with the crowd (be controlled) or seek to control others. Most teens are introduced to self-centered, rebellious and independent attitudes through peers, music and movies sometimes leading to unhealthy behaviors such as cutting, anorexia, bulimia, drugs or alcohol abuse as ways to react to personal struggles with things such as dissatisfaction with their looks, body type or their home life.

Parents who desire their children to form harmonious and encouraging relationships with siblings and peers can start by modeling the characteristics of differentiation. Another way to model differentiation in your home is to affirm each child as a masterpiece who has been created in the image of God. Parents can do this by helping their children to discover their godly bents (Proverbs 22:6).

Children may have academic, athletic, musical, engineering, faith or artistic bents. Parents who draw these bents out of their children will help them to discover how to use them as witnesses of God's goodness and love. These bents allow children to recognize the godly characteristics within them. Parents are responsible to communicate that their children are loved for who they are rather through accomplishments, intelligence or popularity.

Children in the Values stage will naturally want to imitate their parents' personal characteristics. Parents want this type of influence upon their children's lives.

Spiritual Identity

The following table will help parents develop the spiritual identities of their children as examples of differentiation:

The cultural view of children	The biblical view of children
Children are good.	Children are made in the image of God (good), but they have a sin nature.
Children are a by-product of love.	Children are a gift from God.
Family should be a democracy (majority rules).	Children should be given many choices, but parents are the final authority.
Behavior is the highest good.	Character is the highest good
Identity and value are based upon children's accomplishments, such as academics and athletics.	Identity and value are determined by God as our Father and Creator.
The home is one of many important environments in children's lives. Other environments are equal to the home.	Home is the center of family life.

Children who understand their spiritual identities will naturally live out differentiated lifestyles. Christians have received the Holy Spirit, who serves as Counselor and a guiding presence in their lives (John 14:25–27). Parents are responsible to raise their children to know and understand that they belong to God and not to the world (1 Corinthians 6:19–20).

The following Scriptures will substantiate the value of differentiation in a Christian context:

- Romans 12:2: Christians are able to discern God's will for their personal lives.

- 1 Corinthians 2:12: Christians have not received the spirit of the world.

- 2 Corinthians 10:3–4: Christians have been given weapons that will defeat the spirit of the world.

These principles of differentiation will help parents to focus on the strengths of family members. Parents who emphasize strengths rather than weaknesses in children's lives will assist in developing healthy behaviors and emotional wellness in family members (Friedman, 1985). Christian values are catalysts for developing shared identities (differentiation).

Each family member has been given the Holy Spirit, who brings unity into family relationships. Family members are not only connected by blood or marriage (stepfamily), foster care or adoption, but through each person's relationship with God. While each family member is part of a whole, their identity comes from trusting in Christ's atonement in a personal way (Balswick, 2003). Jesus died for all. However, each person must receive him as Savior and Lord in order to discover their true identity (differentiation).

The following Scriptures will help you identify the spiritual gifts and fruits of the Holy Spirit in your children: Romans 12:3–8, 1 Corinthians 12:4–11 and Galatians 5:22–26. The family is the best environment for children and parents to discover what is good and life-giving about each other. Use the table below to identify the spiritual gifts and fruits of the Spirit in your children:

Gift/Fruit of the Spirit	Child's name	Practical application: How does your child express these gifts to other family members? And how do family members benefit from these characteristics?
Peace		
Love		

Joy		
Patience		
Kindness		
Discernment		
Wisdom		
Compassion		
Service		

Shared Values

The values in the right column of the table below will help parents to establish healthy identities in their children's lives also known as differentiation. Parents want to avoid modeling any of the behaviors in the left column which hinder differentiation in their children's identities (Kastner & Wyatt, 2002).

Avoid these behaviors	Promote these values
Parents overcompensate for not being close to their family of origin by smothering their child with attention or affection.	God is the head of your household. God did not give us a spirit of fear but of love, power and self-discipline (2 Timothy 1:7).
An anxious parent can create stress in his/her child. Healthy boundaries are often missing.	Healthy boundaries, such as being respectful of each other's personal space, emotions, bodies, etc. give children an opportunity to experience differentiation between parents and siblings.

Positioning your child to be a hero – your children are always expected to excel.	Safe place for children to succeed and fail. Children need to know they are loved for who they are not for what they do.
Positioning your child to be a scapegoat – your child is expected to fail or get into trouble. He/she is locked into this identity in the family system.	Help children to discover freedom from human bents (sin nature) and understand justification in Christ. Believers are judged to be innocent of the penalty of sin.
Positioning your child to be a mascot/comedian who draws attention to him/herself for acceptance or validation.	Help children to discover their spiritual identity to be transformed by the Word of God.

Nurture in the Values Stage (7–12 years)

The table below will help parents to provide nurture for children with competitive or passive personalities. These two types of personalities need different approaches to nurture.

Children who respond to rewards or rules	Children who respond to affection and communication
Children who respond well to rules need to know that they are meeting the expectations of their parents. (Create chore charts and be sure to reward with stickers, allowance, etc.)	Children who are relational (noncompetitive) need to know when they will have time alone with parents. (Mark the calendar with date nights or special events.)
Parents need to express appreciation and demonstrate affection, especially to children who have bents toward rewards or rules, because they tend to become independent and develop high standards in life.	Parents need to ensure that children with these bents are able to respond to competitive environments, such as school, sports, etc. Children who are relational may not respond to teachers or coaches who try to motivate them to excel through personal challenge or competitive techniques.

Family Mission Statement

The values section of the PAC Model allows parents to establish a family mission statement, for example:

Our family values respect, responsibility, faith, kindness and servanthood and has lots of fun.

Disciplinary measures are based upon neglected values. The consequences for being disrespectful, irresponsible, mean-spirited or self-centered will result in loss of privileges, natural consequences, restrictions and restitution, as needed.

The LIMRI measures shared values in the home. Parents respond to a series of statements, such as:

- I spend an appropriate amount of quality time with our children.

- Our children show me respect.

- Our children respond positively to my discipline.

Couples who disagree with statements like these will receive worksheets that offer spiritual and practical help that enriches their family mission statements.

Improvement Needed Worksheet

The following worksheet is an example of an Improvement Needed Worksheet. The Scriptures, Principles, Discussion Questions and Practical Applications will give spiritual and practical examples to parents seeking growth in these areas.

Worksheet – Conflicting Parenting Styles
Couple agrees improvement is needed.

Statement: Parenting styles are a source of conflict in our marriage.

* Wife agrees with: "Parenting styles are a source of conflict in our marriage."
* Husband agrees with: "Parenting styles are a source of conflict in our marriage."

Scripture

Please meditate on the Scripture below for two days, then answer the following questions.

Proverbs 22:6 NKJV: "Train up a child in the way he should go, and when he is old he will not depart from it."

Participants: Husband, Wife, Coach

What key words or phrases in this Scripture are relevant to you and your relationship with your husband?

Participants: Husband, Wife, Coach

How can this Scripture apply to the statement: "Parenting styles are a source of conflict in our marriage."

Principles

* Proverbs 22:6 teaches parents to model a lifestyle that is Christ-centered.
* Parents are responsible to raise their children to be like Jesus.

* Each child is a unique gift from God and, as a result, may respond to a parenting style that differs from the one used with other children in your family.
* Children need to receive equally from their mother and father.

Participants: Husband, Wife, Coach

Select the principle that is most relevant to you.

Participants: Husband, Wife, Coach

How does this principle apply to your life and relationship with your spouse?

Discussion Question

How are your parenting styles influenced by those used by your parents?
Participants: Husband, Wife, Coach
How does this discussion question apply to your life and relationship with your spouse?

Practical Application

Discuss the following information on parenting styles. Identify the style that you and your spouse most often use with the children. Ask each other how you can balance your parenting styles and identify potential conflicts. All parenting styles have positive and negative aspects to them. There is not one best parenting style. Couples who understand the extremes in their parenting style can rely on their spouse to help them eliminate setting standards too high for the children or being too structured for the children.

- Dominance parenting style: Direct, defined lines of authority. Family works best when leadership is clearly established.
- Influence parenting style: Relational; parenting emphasis is "fun." Family works best when parents are engaged in all phases of the children's lives.
- Steady parenting style: Orderly. Family works best when everyone understands their responsibilities to one another.
- Conscientious parenting style: High standard. Family works best when honesty, integrity and respect are extended toward each other.

Participants: Husband, Wife, Coach

Select the parenting style that best describes you: Dominance, Influence, Steady or Conscientious.

Husband's & Wife's response

List at least three benefits your children receive from your parenting styles.

Participants: Husband, Wife, Coach

List at least three benefits that your spouse brings into your children's lives.

Participants: Husband, Wife, Coach

List at least three extremes in each of your parenting styles, such as too high of a standard or too little discipline.

Participants: Husband, Wife, Coach

Make a commitment to eliminate these extremes by supporting each other's commitment to give your best to your children.

Couple's Worksheet Section (to be completed together)

Husband's Improvement Questions

Participants: Husband, Wife, Coach

Husband asks Wife: "What type of changes can we make to reduce conflicts over our parenting styles?"

Husband asks Wife: "How can I make it better?"
Give one or two examples that are measurable, reasonable and repeatable.

How can these changes enhance your relationship?

Wife's Improvement Questions

Participants: Husband, Wife, Coach

Wife asks Husband: "What type of changes can we make to reduce conflicts over our parenting styles?"

Wife asks Husband: "How can I make it better?"

Give one or two examples that are measurable, reasonable and repeatable.

How can these changes enhance your relationship?

CHAPTER FOUR

Mutuality

Nurture	Values	**Mutuality**	Interdependence
0–6 years	7–12 years	**13–18 years**	19–27 years

This stage of the Parenting Model fosters mutuality between parents and adolescent children. The term "mutuality" will have different reference points for parents. For some, mutuality means equal power and authority. For others, mutuality will mean fair distribution of resources and opportunities. In the context of parenting, I want you to think of mutuality as reciprocity or dependence between family members. Mutuality does not mean that parent and child are equal in maturity or leadership in the home.

The Christian faith requires people to respond to each other from the position of mutual submission (Ephesians 5:21). The primary reason why Christians submit to one another is because everyone has been given a deposit of the Holy Spirit. The Holy Spirit allows each person to represent the love, power, wisdom and holiness of God. Each person represents a vital part of the body of Christ in family or church relationships (Romans 12:3–8).

Christians are not born into the Kingdom of God but adopted into the universal family of God. Each Christian becomes a brother or sister to every other believer in Christ Jesus. This means that siblings are not defined solely as belonging to the same family of origin. All familial relationships are secondary to the fact that all believers are united to each other as brothers and sisters in Christ Jesus. Parents are raising children who will become their brothers and sisters in Christ. Parents and children share the same Father. Jesus is Savior and Lord of each family member.

River Rafting

In my opinion, the experiences of daily parenting responsibilities can be compared to a family rafting trip. The journey downriver begins the day your child comes home from the hospital, or with the first home visit of fostering or adoption.

Most rivers have stretches of slow and fast-moving waters. While enjoying slow waters, family members can sit back and enjoy the ride. Even though rivers appear to be moving slowly, thousands of gallons of water is flowing beneath the raft. In these sections of the river, parent's easily maneuver their rafts using their paddles as rudders. It takes very little effort in lazy sections of the river to float safely between its banks.

At other times, water flow is moving faster and family members need to paddle in unison to keep the boat heading downstream, bow first. As riverbanks become narrower and steeper, water flow increases, and rafts pick up speed. In these sections of the river, parents and children need to have all paddles in the water, steering away from logjams, boulders or jagged rocks.

Parents may feel as if they have lots of time to instill family values and godly behaviors in their children's lives because the pace of life feels manageable and rewarding. In times like these, parents often feel in control of the daily events that occur within their children's lives, especially in the nursery and preschool ages.

Parents quickly discover how their children become influenced both positively and negatively by child-care workers, neighbors, teachers and classmates. Parents ask: "Where did my little one learn that word or behavior?" At this point parents begin the long journey of addressing any residual negativity as a result of unhealthy values and influences that are contrary to their family values.

Children are like barometers, and these behaviors or attitudes reflect their environments. Children respond immediately to stress or anger, as well as to nurture and love. Parents must be intentional and creative in establishing the values of nurture, love and discipline into their children's lives as early as nursery and preschool years.

The same intentionality and creativity is needed for preparing to take your children on rafting trips. River guides launch in calm sections of the river because some training needs to be hands-on, such as learning to back-paddle, paddling in unison and how to recover someone who falls out of the raft.

As river guides, parents may feel as if they have lots of time to prepare children for any upcoming or unexpected dangers that are common with rafting. However, each new season brings spring rains or winter storms, washing trees into the water creating new challenges such as logjams while erosion carves new channels making the river unfamiliar and unpredictable. Parents must never forget that life changes as quickly in family life as on rivers.

Parents grew up in a different worldview and culture than their children. Even though it does not seem possible, cultural and family values of one generation may be lost in the very next generation. The things that parents did as children may never be something their children can do, such as walk to baseball practice or be dropped off at the mall to enjoy a movie.

In one turn of the river, your family can face a series of rapids that were not on the map a year earlier. Parents do not have time to prepare their children for such unpredictable changes in the culture. In these circumstances parents will quickly realize that some of their children's behaviors or attitudes need immediate correction in order to counteract cultural values that are inconsistent with Scriptures or godly character.

These changes do not always imply that your children are rebellious. However, the water's velocity and upcoming rapids require parents to be more intense in their approaches to offset any negative cultural values. At these times, parents need each child to paddle and listen to their instruction without hesitation in order to safely navigate through the rapids. At moments like these, parents need everyone working together in order to steer around potential dangers.

The problems or dangers that were present as parents were growing up are escalated in their children's lives; especially due to the impact of the internet. Today's children are subject to online bullying, pornography, and child predators. Parents were confronted with similar issues but not from the safety of their bedrooms. The loss of respect for teachers, police and political leaders cause children to wonder who can be trusted.

Perhaps the greatest difference between generations is the overwhelming amount of information that floods into your children's minds. Children are being bombarded by cultural struggles in various forms of media. Information about bombings, bullying, drug or alcohol abuse, fatherlessness, abductions, school violence and teen pregnancy rates are streaming into your children's lives in such detail and with such frequency that life becomes overwhelming and frightening.

Parents understand the dangers of rapids and logjams, but children may be caught up in the excitement of bouncing off of the boulders rather than trying to navigate around them. At these times, parents need to be firm and direct due to potential threats to their children's safety. Sometimes children interpret these parental warnings as being controlling rather than life-giving because the culture creates mistrust in parent-child relationships.

Another reason for firm and direct communication is the increase of ambient noise that drowns out parental voices. Many voices are streaming into children's minds, making it difficult for parents' voices to stand out above the other influences, such as cultural trends, friends and media. These types of circumstances require children to respond immediately to avoid flipping the raft or being swept under a logjam. In these times, children may respond to their parent's instructions by asking, "Why do I have to paddle so much and stay in sync with everyone else in the family?"

For the most part, teens do not enjoy being ordered around, especially when everything seems to be okay to them. However, parents view the river (culture) differently from their children. They understand that their children can be thrown from the raft at any moment, facing the possibility of injury or drowning. Parents need to be proactive by talking to their children, especially during the preteen years, about how Christian and cultural values may clash during the journey downriver.

The value of mutuality will serve families well at these times. Parents who model mutuality in their homes are preparing their teens to guide their own raft (life) and future family downriver. The best approach is allowing teens to pilot the family raft in sections of the river that are manageable, before they need to do it on their own.

Some families face rapids every morning. Parents need to have all paddles in the water in order to get everyone off to school. Mornings can turn into rescue missions unless family members stay in sync with each other.

Parental instructions become very direct during rescue missions. At these times children feel confused and stop listening. In their confusion they start asking why and how questions, when in that moment, their parents need obedience in order to avoid danger. Teens may not recognize dangers associated with an increase of water flow moving beneath them. From the viewpoint of a teen everything appears as if their parents are being unreasonable or controlling. Families who do not paddle together at these critical moments run the risk of being overturned with family members spread out on both sides of the river.

Any experienced river guide will seek information from the forest service, other professional guides, as well as asking people who live along the river about water conditions before setting out with inexperienced people in their rafts. The same is true for parents. They should seek advice from other seasoned parents and pastors who have raised children into adulthood. As parents seek guidance they will gain valuable information and resources to navigate these seasons of life as safely and successfully as possible.

Parents seeking wisdom from trusted friends, clergy and counseling professionals will be prepared to identify obstacles (cultural values) that have the potential to threaten biblical and family values.

These conversations will help parents transition from stage one of the PAC Model to the next by finding practical, age appropriate ways to develop nurture, values, mutuality and interdependence in their children. The benefits of each stage of the PAC Model will help children to become disciplined and learn that parents are trusted resources for them to seek counsel as they make choices that will affect their lives far into the future.

Make a list of the daily activities or events where your children need to respond to parental authority in order to be in sync (paddling) with you and other family members.

- Mornings: Getting ready for school
- Evenings: Homework and bedtime
- Weekends: Extracurricular activities, visiting biological parent (stepfamily), etc.

I hope this illustration will help parents see how their responsibilities can change very quickly based on the ages of their children and ever-changing cultural values.

Parenting and Pastoring

Parents with children in the Mutuality stage need to serve as both parent and pastor to their adolescent children. Unfortunately, many parents are unaware of the dual calling in their lives.

These two offices or roles became separated in the fourth century when church leaders made a distinction between clergy and laity. The clergy became responsible for spiritual matters in the lives of their parishioners. One of the negative outcomes of this separation led to parents abdicating the spiritual growth of their children's lives to the church. I believe that parental authority has suffered greatly due to the loss of spiritual authority that came about from these sacred and secular designations.

Today, if you ask parents to identify their main responsibilities, you would most likely hear things like:

1. Meeting the physical and emotional needs of their children;
2. Ensuring they have the best education possible;
3. Helping children to discover their place in life and society;
4. Helping children to become happy and responsible adults.

Unfortunately, you rarely hear things like:

1. Teaching children the difference between righteousness and unrighteousness,
2. Teaching them to worship,
3. Modeling giving to the poor,
4. Modeling serving others, and
5. Modeling confession and repentance from sin.

These matters have been given over to churches. However, anything regarding life and godliness that has been abdicated to churches will become less and less evident in modern culture. Church attendance has not increased over the last several decades and young adults are less likely to be affiliated with religious organizations (Pew Research Center, 2012). It would be safe to say that God always intended the home to be the primary place where children received instruction on all matters of life and godliness (2 Peter 1:3).

Pastors are given the responsibility to turn sinners from pathways of destruction and to equip the saints for the work of ministry (Ephesians 4). Good pastors are concerned with pointing sinners toward righteousness and truth without condemning or shaming them. These types of pastors rejoice when someone repents and turns toward God. Pastors want their disciples to experience the forgiveness, mercy and grace of a loving Father.

Teens benefit greatly from parents who understand how to pastor them during adolescence. Parents who serve as pastors to their adolescent children will have many opportunities to direct them away from sin and self-centeredness that leads to entitlement and self-absorption and onto pathways of servanthood, righteousness and peace with God.

The Bible gives specific instructions for parents and pastors:

Instructions to parents	Instructions to pastors
Tell them of God's goodness and holiness as you experience it in your lives. Psalms 78	Feed my sheep. John 21:17
Teach your children to desire what is good to fill their lives with goodness. Proverbs 22:6	Watch over my flock. John 10:13–15
Do not exasperate your children. Ephesians 6:4	Equip the saints. Ephesians 4:12–13
Be generous. Luke 11:5–13	Lead well. Luke 6:37–41

Pastors are needed most when their disciples are struggling with temptation or trials or have fallen into sin. It is a great honor to be sought out by parishioners when they have sinned but now desire to honor God through repentance and obedience to his Word.

I learned a valuable lesson while serving as a youth pastor that can be useful to parents of adolescents. My wife and I found ourselves parenting many of the teens in our first pastorate. Parents would drop off their teens in the church parking lot, but never enter the doors of the church.

Some of these parents dropped their teens off at our house if conflicts could not be resolved at home. My wife and I were more than willing to open up our home to ensure that teens had a safe place to experience a night or two of peace, prayer and encouragement. Unfortunately, as pastors we became less influential in their lives due to being viewed as parental authorities.

Something totally unexpected happened when teens began to view us as parents rather than their pastors. The more trouble they got into, the less they would seek us out. These teens began to hide their failures from us when they did something wrong. They would go to another pastor to confess their sins out of fear and shame of letting us down. Barbara and I learned that it was important to let teens know that their struggles would never change our love and commitment to help them serve God.

Parents need to tell their teens that one of their responsibilities is to pastor them as well as being moms and dads. Pastors are a sinner's best friend, because they help them to turn away from destructive behaviors and to walk with God in faith and obedience. Parents who are willing to pastor their teens will find many opportunities to direct them away from destructive behaviors and into the arms of a loving and forgiving Father. Teens will find it comforting to know that their parents also need the forgiveness of a loving God.

Parenting by Intuition or Expertise

Currently, many parents are increasingly dependent on the opinions of experts. At one time, parenting was fairly instinctive. But now many parents need the input of specialists to understand their children's need for nurture, values, social, emotional and spiritual development. I believe these trends are being fueled by the medical field that has become very specialized (Friedman, 2007).

Today, general medical practitioners will see you as a patient. Many doctors ask about symptoms rather than learning about the patient. Most patients are referred to specialists who have another process of diagnosis. Many medical procedures are no longer treated by doctors that know your personal life, family history and work environments. The specialist will either perform the needed procedure or refer you to a surgeon who know even less about you.

Parents rely less on their instincts and seek information from books or websites that inform them on how to do things that were once passed down from generation to generation. One of the major contributors in the loss of parental confidence is due to the breakdown of family life such as divorce, never-married parents or single-parent homes. Many parents do not have confidence in themselves or their parents (grandparents) to pass down proven parental care and biblical values.

Parents can be confident, because their authority comes from God. God has empowered every parent to extend grace, mercy, justice and love to their children on his behalf.

Restrictive and Permissive Parenting Styles

At one time, the terms "restrictive" and "permissive" parenting represented traditional parenting styles in academia. Permissive parenting describes parents who focus on the child's need for nurture and security. Parents who fall into the category of restrictive parenting are thought to prioritize a child's need for discipline and self-control. Recently, educators and sociologists have changed these terms to mean control (restrictive) and support (permissive) (Balswick, 2003).

The following table will help parents to assess what experts are saying about these different parenting styles. Christian parents are responsible to develop parenting strategies that are based upon biblical values. I would like you to consider the benefits of an Authoritative parenting style. The following comparisons come from a study by Diana Baumrind (Grobman, 2003–2008):

Style	Description	Discipline
Authoritative	An Authoritative style is high in control and high in support. High in control means parents are present in all areas of children's lives. High in support means that parents prioritize the characteristics of nurture with their children.	An Authoritative style of discipline typically endorses judicious ways to discipline children that may include spanking "but in a context of a warm, engaged and relational parent-child relationship." I believe that spanking should be the last option in redirecting unhealthy behaviors in a child's life. I hope that parents use spanking as a last form of discipline and very sparingly. Studies show that corporal punishment is not the most effective means of discipline and needs to be combined with other types of discipline.
Authoritarian	An Authoritarian style is low in support and high in control. Low in support means that parents prioritize the characteristics of submission rather than nurture with their children. High in control means that parents make most of the decisions for their children. Children may struggle to think for themselves with this style of parenting.	An Authoritarian style of discipline will reflect the standards of the parent. The parent's values become the standard rather than the Scriptures. Children who feel as if they are failing their parents will fall into two categories: 1) They do not feel as if they will ever measure up to their parents' standards. 2) They will stop trying to please their parents and become rebellious or judgmental toward their parents.

Permissive	A Permissive style is high in support and low in control. High in support prioritizes the characteristics of nurture at the expense of control. Low in control means that children are self-directed. They are not given boundaries to guide their behaviors and attitudes.	A Permissive style of discipline will typically focus on positive redirection, time out and verbal communication. Parents want to be close to their children and do not want discipline to create distance or discord between them. This style of discipline will fall short when these disciplinary measures do not bring the child to repentance. Children have a sin nature that requires repentance rather than behavior modification.

Kastner and Wyatt prefer parenting styles that favor a more relational model. The role of a parent may need to go from chief executive officer (decision maker) to consultant in order to keep adolescents from leaning toward independence (Kastner & Wyatt, 2002). I believe the transition from CEO to consultant (empowering others to become critical thinkers) will allow adolescents to embrace the values of mutuality and interdependence. Problem solving is one of the greatest gifts that parents can give to their children. Consultants are sought out when important decisions need to be made in areas that need a cost-to-benefit analysis. Parents want to become more like consultants to their children between the ages of nineteen to twenty-seven.

Parenting Styles

Steven Mintz identifies three perceptions that dictate the way parents raise their children. The Premodern (Colonial era) phase perceives children as adults in training. The second, Modern phase (1800's – early 1900's), perceives children as dependent upon their parents and needing their protection. The third, Postmodern phase (late 1900's), perceives children through a consumer culture that struggles to define gender roles, family values and morals (Balswick & Balswick, 2014).

Parents need to understand that family systems theory is based upon scientific approaches to relationships, cultures and societies. However, parenting is not a science. Parenting is a relationship between adults and children who are in various stages of maturity. Each person is learning to overcome their sinful bents through the power of the Holy Spirit. Parents are modeling what it means to be a nonanxious presence in their children's lives that fosters differentiation between siblings and as future spouses and parents.

What Creates Generational Gaps?

Parents need to understand what fuels the generational gap between adolescents and adulthood. In the United States, adolescence is an intricate part of its cultural identity. However, many cultures outside of the U.S. recognize teens as young adults. Some of these cultures invite teenagers into adulthood around the age of thirteen. These young men and women are not given full adult responsibilities, but they are pointed toward adulthood earlier in their lives than most American teens.

American teenage culture is influenced by corporations and the profit motive, more specifically. Corporations have fueled the generational gap between adolescents and adulthood (Lapowsky, 2014). Teenagers have become sources of revenue for many businesses. These corporations market their food, clothing, music and technology to adolescents in order to establish long-term relationships with them. It is very common to see young adults up to age thirty wearing the same clothes, listening to the same music, using the same technology and eating at the same restaurants that were primarily teen markets.

I believe that adolescent culture has been propagated by corporations that desire to keep them as clients for at least twenty years. My experiences as a pastor over the last twenty-five years shows that adolescent value systems can stretch into the late twenties and early thirties.

Many young adults are stuck in adolescent mindsets because they have not learned to make decisions using a cost-to-benefit analysis.

Many of the struggles that young married couples face are related to adolescent values that do not translate well into marriage or parental relationships and responsibilities. Young married couples commonly experience conflicts over the amount of time that is spent playing video games, hanging out with single friends, gambling online or continuing to vacation with friends that existed before their relationship started.

Parents who invite their adolescent children into mutually respectful and responsible family relationships will be able to counteract many of the secular values that create a stasis of adolescent values. The type of stasis that I am referring to is borrowed from the sci-fi genre. Stasis is a type of deep sleep where space travel requires decades to achieve its destination. Our culture invites teens into a holding pattern of adolescence that can last into their early thirties. One of the primary goals of parenting is to prepare adolescent children to become responsible and respectful spouses and parents.

Nurture in the Mutuality Stage (13–18 years)

Parents need to adjust quickly to their teens' openness or resistance toward nurture. Teens will cuddle up to their parents for a moment, creating a yearning for days gone by when physical affection was a normal expression of nurture and love. These moments can fade quickly, leaving parents wondering if they have done something wrong. Be encouraged. It is normal behavior for adolescents to bounce between expressing physical affection and being independent.

The table below will help to develop appropriate types of nurture between parents and teens. Some teens are inclined to connect easily with parents, while others question the relevance of their parent's values of family life. Parents who learn new and creative ways to express nurture during their children's adolescence will help them to stay connected to them throughout their adult years.

Teens who ally themselves to their parents	Teens who become suspicious of their parents' relevance
Teens who ally themselves to their parents need to be involved in family decisions and choices. Parents need to ensure that their teens can stand alone in their convictions, because it will not be long before they enter college or the workforce.	Teens who are suspicious of their parents' relevance need to be given permission to challenge decisions and choices that affect family life. Parents need to adopt a "respectful dialogue" practice with teens. Respectful dialogue means expressing a different opinion or value respectfully.

Mutuality

Mutuality is caught more than taught. The LIMRI statements that measure mutuality in married and engaged relationships include:

- I am able to talk with my spouse about things that we disagree on.
- I am quick to forgive my spouse.
- I don't alienate my spouse when we have a conflict.
- I am respectful of my spouse's ideas.
- I treat my spouse as a coequal.
- I resolve conflicts with my spouse quickly.
- I listen to my spouse's point of view when we disagree.

Children will benefit greatly from parents who model these characteristics. Place a minus sign (-) next to statements that you model infrequently. Plan to work on statements that were marked with a minus sign by meeting with a counselor or pastor.

CHAPTER FIVE

Interdependence

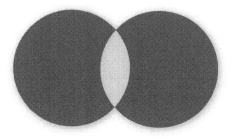

Nurture	Values	Mutuality	Interdependence
0–6 years	7–12 years	13–18 years	19–27 years

The Interdependence stage of the PAC Model will help prepare adult children to become mature spouses, parents and disciples. Not every adult will become a spouse. However, studies show that ninety percent of young adults expect to marry during their lifetime (Agence France-Presse, 2012).

Financial Pressure

Currently, up to 5.9 million young adults between the ages of twenty-five and thirty-four live with their parents (Mather, 2011). College graduates average up to $25,000 of student loan debt, an increase of five percent from 2009 (Pope, 2012).

The increase in student debt and fewer manufacturing jobs limits opportunities for young adults to live on their own. These trends make in necessary for parents to help their adult children. At the same time, many parents feel the strain of the 2008 economic downturn on their personal finances. Adult children and parents who find themselves living under one roof need to develop a common understanding of the pressures that each person faces in these economic times in order to form a mutually encouraging and supportive home life.

Parents can reduce relational challenges and financial pressures of adult children living with them by following these steps:

1. Establish written agreements with adult children living in your home that establishes timelines such as six months to one year. Once residency has been established, it is difficult to remove an adult child from your home.

2. Charge rent. Parents can choose to return the money to help their adult child to move into an apartment, pay off credit card debt, or student loans. Parents can also use the money to offset their expenses for additional costs in food and utilities (Silver-Greenberg, 2011).

3. Map out financial and home management plans with your adult children that include lists of chores and timelines to complete them (Thom Fox in Silver-Greenberg, 2011).

These suggestions will help parents to focus on the most important aspects of supporting their adult children through spiritual conversations, problem solving and friendship.

Decision Making

Currently, the average age of men and women getting married is between twenty-six and twenty-eight years of age (Cherlin, 2010). This trend allows young adults to benefit from conversations with their parents about decisions that married couples typically make together. Many young adults are buying homes or new cars, moving to another state or making career choices without spouses to help them assess pros and cons of these life-changing decisions.

Parents have wonderful opportunities to become advocates for their adult children in making decisions about careers, education, home buying and relationships that will affect them far into the future.

Many dating relationships end abruptly when boy/girlfriends are asked to participate in decisions that far outweigh the commitment levels of their relationships. Only fiancé's, spouses or parents can be trusted in decisions that have the potential to affect someone's future, credit rating, or career paths. Parents have unique opportunities to listen, share advice and pray for these types of decisions with their adult children.

Jack and Judith Balswick explain that empowerment is not giving away some of your parental power to your adult children (Balswick & Balswick, 2014). True empowerment occurs as parents encourage their adult children to make decisions in crucial areas such as spiritual growth, careers, and education with cost-to-benefit analysis.

Anything less than this type of empowerment can lead to enmeshment or codependence between adult children and their parents.

Parents are well positioned to become a non-anxious presence in these critical areas of their adult children's lives. However, parents must avoid triangulation into the anxiousness of their adult children's decision-making process. If this happens, relationships between parents and adult children will struggle due to unrealistic expectations on both parts about life-changing decisions. Adult children are fully responsible to make personal decisions and choices that will lay the foundation of wise stewardship over their finances, careers, relationships and talents.

Many parents may feel uncomfortable with these discussions because their own parents did not make themselves available or were unwilling to be involved at this stage of their lives (19–27 years). The motto, "the American way," is a testament of individualism which means trusting in yourself. This ideology, which celebrates becoming your own man or woman without input from others, has not served young adults well over the last twenty years. Many young married couples struggle with smothering debt loads and risky financial and career choices that have long-term consequences on their relationships.

Parents with children in the Interdependence stage should not make decisions for their children. However, they should make themselves available to pray and discuss options with them when asked. Parents are more likely to be invited to participate in these types of decisions by avoiding any temptations to control outcomes or possible failures that may result in their adult children choices.

Relational Differentiation

As discussed in chapter three, differentiation is essential in forming interdependent relationships with adult children. The LIMRI measures relational differentiation in married and engaged relationships.

Some of these statements include:

- I am not passive-aggressive with my anger toward my spouse.
- I repent quickly when I am wrong.
- I resolve conflicts quickly with my spouse.
- I am successful at prioritizing our relationship.
- I share spiritual insights with my spouse.

Parents who transfer these qualities of relational differentiation into their relationships with adult children will lay the foundation of interdependence and friendship. Place a plus sign (+) next to the statements above that you model frequently with your children and a minus sign (-) next to statements that are modeled infrequently. What can you do to begin modeling any statements that were marked as infrequent or never in relationship to your children?

How Young Adults See Themselves

Parents often view their unmarried adult children as singles who will one day be married. However, many nineteen to twenty-seven year olds do not think of themselves as single because unlike previous generations, a smaller percentage of men and women expect to be married before age thirty (Cherlin, 2010).

Most likely young adults of past generations thought of themselves as single adults in their early to mid-twenties because the culture defined them in this way. However, this is no longer the case. Today's young adults do not see themselves as being married or having children until they own homes and establish career paths. The desire to raise a family is still a priority, but it does not come into play until later in life. The parents who currently have adult children were most likely already married and parenting at the current ages of these children.

In past generations, marriage was viewed as a pathway into adulthood. This cultural distinction became clear to me on a missions trip to Zambia, where I taught on marriage and family life. Zambians still view marriage as the pathway into adulthood. You are fully embraced as an adult following your wedding day. Even though Americans do not have this cultural tradition, we may have an internal bent that affects the way we look at single adults and adulthood.

Young adults have many legitimate reasons for their reservations about becoming spouses and parents. The divorce culture negatively influences the way young adults think about marriage. Many of them struggle to understand the purpose of marriage due to the loss of healthy marriages within their extended families. Marriage is no longer the highest goal for many couples. Couples often choose to cohabit in order to avoid the devastating effects of divorce. Unfortunately, cohabiting couples have divorce rates up to twenty-five percent higher than noncohabiting couples (Cherlin, 2010).

The suspicion of young adults toward marital success has become known as "capstone marriage." Capstone marriages occur once cohabiting couples complete their education, establish careers and have children (Cherlin, 2010). At one time marriage was the foundation that thrusted young couples toward their futures. Today, capstone marriages are symbols of successful lives.

Many young adults have lost two generations of marriages in their families since the passing of No-Fault Divorce legislation in 1969. Today's young adults not only experienced divorce between parents but also grandparents and aunts and uncles.

The PAC Model will help parents model relationship skills that can be emulated in their adult children's dating, engaged or marriage relationships. Many of the people who become friends, boy/girlfriends or fiancés to your adult children will be unfamiliar with the values that defined your home. However, the good news is that eighty-eight percent of people surveyed in the U.S. agree that couples who marry should make lifelong commitments to each other (Glenn, 2005). These couples also feel that American culture would be better off if divorce were harder to attain. The children of divorce desire more stability in their relationships than their parents were able to maintain.

Benefits of Adult Children Living at Home

There are many advantages to parents and adult children living in one household. An interdependent relationship between parent and adult child includes growing closer as brothers and sisters in Christ. Parents will benefit in many ways from the spiritual vitality and challenges that come with adult children living in their homes.

The following table will help parents to develop interdependent relationships with their adult children.

Benefits of parenting child into adulthood beyond age eighteen	Costs to child development when parents abandon parenting roles/responsibilities at age eighteen.
Allows parents to model long-term commitments to their adult children's success.	Adult children feel that their parents have a limited interest in their lives. Parents are counting down the years until they are no longer responsible for their child.
Parents can offer support and counsel when an adult child makes poor or good decisions.	Adult child may not share their successes or seek counsel when they make poor decisions.
Parents will actively pray for specific areas of their adult children's lives that they are struggling to overcome.	Adult children are left to make important decisions without parents having an opportunity to offer advice or pray for them.
Allows parents to communicate how they overcame mistakes and poor choices during their young adult years.	Adult child may have to learn from their own mistakes without the benefit of discussing how parents overcame mistakes in their young adult years.

Allows parents to communicate their desire to grow spiritually with adult child.	Adult child may feel that spirituality is not something that is shared with parents.
Gives parents an opportunity to repent or apologize for missing the mark when their children were younger.	Adult child may not benefit from renewed relationship with parents as friends who are seeking the Lord together.

Parents will discover greater depths of God's love by establishing nurture, values, mutuality and interdependence with their children.

My interviews with parents revealed many common struggles and blessings associated with parenting adult children. Some of these included:

- Parents struggled with trying to influence the decisions of their adult children rather than encouraging and praying with them about their choices.

- Parents were gripped with fear as their children made poor choices and decisions during the college years. They often tried to rescue their children rather than helping them to embrace the natural consequences of their actions.

- Parents struggled with the length of time it took for their adult children to admit to their poor decisions. However, parents who were able to demonstrate unconditional love toward struggling or prodigal children reported that they eventually showed appreciation for their parents' love and support.

- Parents struggled with separation anxiety as their children went off to college or moved out of the home. Adult children also experienced some separation anxiety during these years.

Parents who spoke encouragement and prayed with their adult children were able to let go of any feelings of personal failure for past rebellious behavior or decisions of their children. These parents were able to support their children as brothers and sisters in Christ, who were struggling to live out the consequences of poor choices or decisions, but with hope of a better future.

The most important things parents can do for their struggling children is to point them to Jesus, who will help them in their trials and tribulations.

Parents empower adult children by sharing their own struggles to overcome poor or unwise decisions, and how submitting to God changed these outcomes. Adult children need to know that their parents struggled with pride, fear, bitterness, injustice or shame. Parents who hide personal failures from their adult children will, inadvertently, make them feel as if they do not measure up when they fail or make poor decisions. However, parents who share these types of personal struggles will help adult children know that they share a desperate need for Jesus.

Parents need to establish a coaching model in their parenting philosophy during these years. Many parents who make the transition to coaching rather than parenting are blessed to watch their children discover God's grace and wisdom. Coaching positions parents to come alongside of their adult children rather than being in front trying to make life work better or behind trying to bolster them up when they face difficult situations.

Coaching allows young adults to discover God as a loving Father who is waiting to be invited into their lives. They will discover that God is patient, faithful, and is present in both their successes and failures. Coaches are always alongside of the person rather than in front leading or behind pushing them.

Successful Parenting vs. Faithful Parenting

Many parents struggle to differentiate between being a successful parent and a faithful parent. Parents want to give their children every opportunity to be successful adults. Perhaps a better description of successful parenting is the word "safe." I believe that many parents are motivated to create safe lives for their children rather than successful lives. The definition of "success" is "a favorable or desired outcome" (Merriam-Webster, 2015). These favorable outcomes are usually associated with money, education, marriage or status. However, success is always associated with some type of risk taking or suffering.

Most parents place a high value on their children's education, athletics, and extracurricular activities to create the safest possible journey toward adulthood. The word "happy" is another way to describe safety. Perhaps the phrase, "Raising happy children," typifies the parenting values of the New Millennium. Parents who fall into this category inadvertently limit as much risk as possible in their children's lives.

Children will not benefit from parents who try to eliminate risks, disappointments or failures in their lives. Parents who are fearful of the future will do everything possible to ensure that their children pass a class, make a sports teams or have lots of friends, even at the expense of natural consequences or character development. These types of opportunities or privileges do not mean that children will experience happiness as adults.

As adults, these children will often resent their parents hovering over their lives. These types of parents are known as "helicopter parents" (Wikipedia, 2014). Helicopter parents have been known to go on job interviews with their adult children to ensure their salaries and benefit packages are acceptable. Parents can find more on the subject of helicopter parents by reading the following authors: Ron Alsop, Madeline Levine and Judith Warner.

The Goal of Parenting

Dennis Kinlaw defines the family as a way for children to discover the meaning of father with a capital "F" (Kinlaw, 2104). He says that family is the key to gaining a right understanding of God. Parents who understand the purpose of family will become faithful parents. The word "faithful" can be described as being "true … to a standard, or to an original" (Merriam-Webster, 2015).

We must ask the question: Why did God create the family? Kinlaw answers this question: "God places us in family because it is what a child needs" (Kinlaw, 2104). The story of the Prodigal Son (Luke 15:11–32) reveals the steps of becoming a faithful parent.

The father was presented with an unusual request from his younger son – to leave the family business and be given a share of his inheritance. This type of request would have been considered as disrespectful and countercultural of first-century family values. The father would be criticized by his peers for his son's behavior. Perhaps the father chose to respond to his son's request in order to create an opportunity to teach him about the father with a capital "F." This was a very risky decision for the father, who gave away a significant source of business capital in order to turn his son away from a hedonistic lifestyle.

Most first-century sons would work alongside of their fathers and learn trades or skills that would one day support their own families. However, the prodigal son rejected family responsibilities by asking for an inheritance. He did not consider the implications to his own family's financial security of such a request.

The prodigal son's dad risked financial security in order to give his son an opportunity to discover the identity and character of a loving father. A scenario such as this could lead to unfavorable outcomes that could potentially push the son further away from his father and deeper into a self-centered lifestyle. However, the father understood his son better than anyone else. He believed this was the only option left to change the prodigal's heart or lose him forever to the world. Perhaps this was the father's last opportunity to point his younger son toward a loving God.

The son quickly squandered his wealth and became homeless. These circumstances created an awareness that his father's servants had plenty of food to eat and warm places to sleep. He envied their lifestyle and rehearsed a strategy to become accepted as one of the hirelings on the family farm. This behavior is indicative of someone seeking personal comfort and happiness. The prodigal son was moving closer to being a responsible adult, but at this point he had more to learn.

The prodigal rehearsed these words:

"I have sinned against heaven and against you. I am no longer worthy to be called your son; make me like one of your hired men" *(Luke 15:18–19).*

These words represented his best plan to satisfy his hunger and homelessness. Perhaps these words represented his best attempt to repent and humble himself before his father. However, his plan reveals an underdeveloped understanding of love, mercy and grace. He only understood life through the lens of self-centeredness and individualism. It appears that he grew up in a generous and stable household. However, he appears to have developed a sense of entitlement.

The story reminds us that godly parents love their children more than their own lives. A faithful parent may be disappointed or grieved over their child's behavior, but he or she will always love them. Faithful parents understand that God's love never fails them (Roman 8:38–39). God chooses to love us as sons and daughters. Many people do not grasp this divine truth: "While we were still sinners, Christ died for us" (Romans 5:8).

Parents who embrace the love of God will develop a type of love for their children that goes beyond human capacities. The goal of every parent should be to develop an unconditional love for their children. I have seen parents stand by their children who have committed heinous crimes, such as murder, dealing drugs and rape. The love that parents have for their children is an expression of God's unconditional love for mankind. Unconditional love does not mean that consequences, boundaries or restitution should be passed over.

Trust and Trustworthiness

The prodigal son understood trust as something that is earned rather than learned. Trust can be restored by an offending person's willingness to repent, submit, restore and make restitution for the consequences of broken trust. Children who steal money from their parent may need to repay the amount that was stolen and do extra chores in order to restore the trust that was broken over the offenses. However, there is a better way to reestablish trust that has been breached.

A "trust that is learned" requires both people in the conflict to play active roles in restoring trust back into the relationship. An untrustworthy person must demonstrate trustworthy behaviors, while the person who was offended must be willing to become trusting in appropriate degrees. In many cases of broken trust, it is more difficult for the victim to become trusting of the offender than for the offender to honor boundaries and repay what was stolen or broken, such as fidelity or integrity. Victims of broken trust must learn to take their pain and disappointments to God in order to have their hearts healed from the weight of these burdens.

The prodigal son may have been contrite in his appeal to earn a place among his father's servants. However, his goal in being a servant rather than a repentant son in his father's household missed the mark. His heart had become hardened by entitlement and self-centeredness. This made it impossible for him to embrace restoration and forgiveness.

Parents must remember that children who do not appreciate them are struggling with their human bents (sin nature). Each child must learn to overcome pride, anger, selfishness, power or control. Faithful parents desire to come alongside of their children in order to help them find healing and discover their identities as children of God.

Parenting and Magnets

Parenting rebellious children can be like working with magnets. Two magnets are unable to form connections when they are placed in their negative polarities. Friction builds as negative polarities move closer to each other.

I have seen this principle at work between parents and children. The negative bents in rebellious children, such as anger or entitlement, will often draw out the negative bents in their parent, such as impatience, judgment and criticism. The friction between parents and children increases as these negative behaviors clash with each other. The frustrated parents may resort to power and control in order to create some type of order in the home. Of course, this usually results in drawing out more anger and entitlement from the children.

Magnets in positive polarities have the same results. I have seen many parent and child relationships struggle when neither side is willing to acknowledge any of their faults. The frustrated child will not admit any of their negative bents, such as anger or entitlement, while the parent refuses to acknowledge using fear or criticism to bring order to the home. The friction between magnets in positive polarities increase as they move closer to each other. The only way to experience healing between parents and children is through acts of confession, repentance and forgiveness.

Magnets form connections when negative and positive polarities are facing each other. Parents must be willing to extend mercy, grace, patience or forgiveness (positive polarity) toward their children when they are struggling with entitlement or anger (negative polarity). Parenting is all about building connections with your children in order to help them overcome their sin natures (negative polarity).

We see this principle at work between the father and his prodigal son. The father sees his son in the distance, walking toward home. He runs to his son, extending mercy and forgiveness (positive polarity). His son confesses his sin (negative polarity) and experiences love and forgiveness. The parenting style of the faithful father teaches us many valuable lessons:

- **The first lesson:** Parents must be willing to celebrate the life of their children. The life that I am describing is what God alone deposits into his children. Too often, parents only celebrate the success of their children, such as academic or athletic rewards or compliance to parental authority. Children will soon learn that they must perform in order to be accepted. Children need to know that their parents love them for who they are, not for what they do or will become as adults. It is essential that parents focus on the uniqueness of their children rather than on any of their failures or successes.

- **The second lesson:** Parents must celebrate the faithfulness of God to preserve his wayward children. As long as your children are alive, there is hope for their salvation and the healing of their souls.

- **The third lesson:** Parents must celebrate when their children accept father with a capital "F." Every parent wants to be loved by their children, but it is more important that they come to love God as Father.

- **The last lesson:** Compliant children can miss what it means to know God as father with a capital "F." The older brother was a compliant child, not asking for favors or his inheritance. He stayed within the acceptable behaviors of the culture. However, he was bitter and allowed a spirit of judgment to fill his heart. He was upset that his father had extended forgiveness and mercy to his brother in the form of a great celebration.

    Even though the younger son received an abundance of forgiveness and mercy, the story does not indicate that he received any additional inheritance. He was not rewarded for his self-centered behavior. However, he was loved with a divine love that would allow him to understand who God is as a father with a capital "F."

Parents must be as intentional in their parenting of compliant children as they would strong-willed or rebellious children. A faithful parent understands the differences between happiness and maturity. Parents who try to give children everything that he or she wants in order to make them happy will not necessarily be raising mature adults. Children must learn that happiness comes from knowing God as their Father and the benefits of delayed gratification.

Parents who follow the PAC Model will give their children head starts in becoming mature disciples and future spouses. Your children will not only reap the rewards of your parenting values, but also be able to identify a future spouse who is prepared to develop relationships that may one day form marriage covenants. I believe that children who receive the benefits of nurture, values, mutuality and interdependence will be prepared to form healthy relationships as adults.

Nurture in the Interdependence Stage (19–27 years)

In chapter three I explained that differentiation is the ability to hold onto a non-anxious presence when facing chaotic environments (Friedman, 1985). Parents have opportunities, through nurturing relationships with their children, to raise non-anxious rather than anxious adult children.

In my experiences as a marriage and family life pastor, anxious adult children are caught in double binds. The marketplace is screaming for entrepreneurial young adults to make significant changes in everything, including tech, education and interpersonal relationships. This age group has been championed as the change agents for the world. These pressures are compounded by a struggling economy, rising educational costs, delays in finding future spouses and fewer job opportunities. Many young adults tend to overthink or doubt their abilities to recover from failures in careers and relationships, and educational debt.

Non-anxious adult children view failures as part of the growth process. New opportunities are catalysts for success. Many of the most successful people throughout history experienced multiple failures, and saw recovery as the pathway to success.

In the table below, parents will find practical ways to form connections with both anxious and non-anxious adult children:

Connecting with anxious adult children	Connecting with non-anxious adult children
Some adults seek advice rather than empowerment. Parents will serve their adult children well by asking: "What is it that you want to accomplish or experience in life?" and: "If you fail, what is at risk?" Parents can help their children to understand that family will always be the measure of success and stability in their lives.	Some adults will become over-focused on success and view relationships with parents and siblings as expendable in order to achieve the cultural values associated with successful careers, education or relationships. Parents need to be intentional in pursuing their non-anxious adult children by being invitational, for example meeting them on their terms for lunch, early coffee or late evening dinners.

The illustrations below, the PAC Model and *Journey to Oneness*, show the progression of covenant relationships (Hitchcock, 2013). The PAC Model instills the attributes of nurture, values, mutuality and interdependence in children's lives in order to equip them to form future covenant relationships in adulthood.

The PAC model equips your children to form adult relationships that embody spiritual identity, friendship, validation, sacrificial love and covenant vows. The values in the PAC Model and Journey to Oneness will equip children to develop healthy marriage relationships.

Parenting your child into adulthood

Age 0–6 years	Age 7–12 years	Age 13–18 years	Age 19–27 years
Nurture	**Values**	**Mutuality**	**Interdependence**
Child is dependent upon parent to develop trust with them.	Child moving forward More flexibility	Adolescent living out choices and natural consequences Push for flexibility	Young adults seeking parental wisdom for choices Balance closeness/ flexibility

Journey to Oneness

Identity	Friendship	Committed Dating	Engaged	Marriage Covenant	Oneness

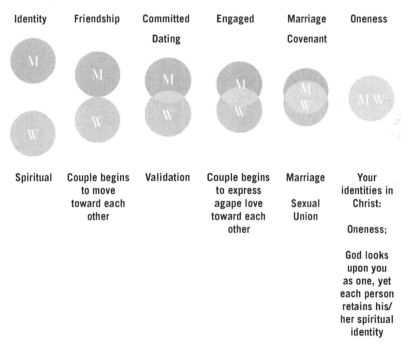

| Spiritual | Couple begins to move toward each other | Validation | Couple begins to express agape love toward each other | Marriage

Sexual Union | Your identities in Christ:

Oneness;

God looks upon you as one, yet each person retains his/ her spiritual identity |

CHAPTER SIX

Friendships with Adult Children

Some parents may be cautious about forming friendships with their adult children. The theology of friendship is modeled after the relationships between Jesus and his followers (John 15:13–15). The characteristics of friendship are:

1. Willingness to lay down one's life for a friend;
2. Commitment to obey God's commands;
3. Sharing all that is good and wise from the Father.

Jesus is the ultimate friend. He laid down his life for everyone at the cross as an example of sacrificial love and friendship (Roman 5:8). His life and death invites everyone who believes in him to love God and others in similar ways (Matthew 22:36–40). Even in his departure from the Earth; he demonstrated his long-term commitment to us by sending the Holy Spirit to be our guide and counselor (John 14:15–21). The life of Christ is lived out in family relationships through sacrificial love, and sharing all that is good and wise with each other. The family is the best environment for children to experience these foundational truths for relationships.

Parents want to consistently model the following characteristics to their children:

1. Parenting is all about sacrificial love. Most parents would gladly lay down their own lives to ensure their children's safety

and health. They do this regularly by prioritizing their children's needs on a daily basis.

2. The primary goal of parenting is to model loving God and loving others.

3. Parents will naturally share all that is good and wise from the Father with their children.

Many cultural shifts over the last twenty years have not proven to be family friendly. However, one of these shifts has given parents opportunities to develop friendships with their adult children. Children are staying longer with their parents, or returning home after college or after failed attempts at living on their own and sometimes with a spouse. These 'homecomings' give parents opportunities to invite their adult children into what God is doing in their lives.

Parents should avoid thinking of these opportunities as second chances to parent their adult children, especially when relationships during the teen years were difficult. Parents are inviting their adult children into new opportunities of relating to one another. Parenting out of guilt, shame or remorse will only make things difficult. However, a time of confession, repentance and forgiveness can be valuable in starting new relationships, especially when parents prioritized careers or relationships over their children's needs. Attempts to reparent may also be triggered if their children were rebellious or resistant to parental love and guidance throughout the elementary or adolescent years. Building interdependent relationships with adult children is not about the past, but the future.

The additional time that parents now have with their adult children is best used to develop mutual faith, respect, responsibility and encouragement. Parents will always be mom and dad to their adult children. But now parents have opportunities to extend the characteristics of friendship and blessing to their adult children. Adult children who need to live with their parents but reject opportunities to engage in faith, respect, responsibility, trust and integrity will need to find other living arrangements.

Adult children typically default to childhood roles and responsibilities in the adjustment period of moving back home. I believe adult children feel as if their parents' lifestyles are somewhat out of reach due to the changes in the economy and fewer entry level jobs that pay enough to support living independently. Home ownerships seems out of reach so they don't aspire to learn how to manage or maintain their parent's home.

One of the achievements that young adults question is marriage relationships. In my opinion, some of the causes of marriage being out of the reach of young adults include:

1. An increasing number of young adults are growing up in single parent or divorced homes.

2. Young adults are waiting longer before considering marriage relationships. The mean age for women is twenty-seven and twenty-nine for men (Cohn, 2013).

3. Career stability for young adults, especially men, takes longer than in previous generations (Carnevale, Hanson & Gulish, 2013).

I believe that this trend of waiting longer for marriage leads to higher levels of independence and resistance to compromise. Parents have great opportunities to discuss in honest and candid ways with adult children what made their relationships healthy or unhealthy. By doing this, parents will help their adult children prepare for future marriage relationships.

In my experiences over the last eighteen years, many premarital couples struggle to understand how dating or marrying someone from a divorced or single-parent home can be more challenging and require additional skills to build shared identities based upon mutuality, emotional honesty and intimacy. Parents can help adult children who are dating someone who is a child of divorce by gathering resources and discussing their personal experiences as well as those of extended family members.

Even though your home may have stayed intact, it is likely that someone in your family has been through a divorce and remarriage. Your children need to understand how children of divorce may struggle to develop emotionally intimate relationships. Parents can recommend that their adult children read the book *The Unexpected Legacy of Divorce* by Wallerstein, Lewis and Blakeslee (2000). This book will help any child of divorce and his/her fiancé to overcome patterns of behavior that can threaten emotional intimacy in marriage relationships.

Many studies and books have identified love, honesty, intimacy, mutuality and accompaniment as essential characteristics of couple satisfaction (Benner, 2002; Foley, 2003; Seligman, 2000). Even though these stages were originally meant to describe marital relationships, I will apply these elements to parenting adult children.

- **Love:** Parents have opportunities to develop bonds of love that go beyond any sense of obligation. The PAC Model allows children to experience sacrificial love in the context of the familial bonds between parent and child.

- **Honesty:** Parents and adult children know each other's strengths and growth areas. Emotional honesty is one of the essential characteristics of long-term relationships. Healthy relationships look for solutions when offenses occur, fostering discussions about subjects that would typically be off limits, such as faith, politics or social justice.

- **Mutuality:** Parents and adult children have opportunities to extend and receive friendship from one another. Typically, friendships are formed over common goals, interests or stages of life. Friendships between parents and adult children begin with deeper intimacy. The vehicle or catalyst for forming friendships is "living together" as adults. Parents and adult children know the best and worst about each other, yet they are learning to respond to each other through a different lens. As adults, each person is learning to look beyond any bias that was formed during the elementary and adolescent years in order to become friends.

- **Accompaniment:** Parents and adult children are supportive of each other's journey through life. Parents add value to their adult children's journey by sharing lessons and insights from personal successes and failures. Some of the best parents that I have met play an important role as encouragers to their adult children. Many adult children feel as if they are underemployed, their earning potentials is too limited, or they are unable to get started in their preferred career fields. Parents can encourage their children not to give up on their dreams. Adult children can add value to their parents' journey by their enthusiasm for life, incorporation of technology and offering new perspectives on cultural trends and the benefits of higher education.

Keeping Adult Children Safe

Many adult children feel trapped between adolescence and adulthood. They often feel a need for more education, job experience or a good break in order to move toward their futures. Parents will serve their children well by paying attention to any signs of behavior associated with depression.

Many adult children feel as if they are falling behind or not measuring up because they are living at home. In some cases, adult children do not want to leave the safety, convenience and benefits of living at home. Parents need to watch for signs of depression in their adult children that may be triggered by limited employment opportunities, earning potential, student loan debt, or struggles with areas of faith in a secularized culture.

The following statements are indicators of depression among young adults:

- I feel sad all the time and just don't feel like myself.

- I don't enjoy being with my friends or doing any of the things I usually love to do.

- I've been having a lot of trouble sleeping lately.

- Sometimes I feel like my life is not worth living anymore.

- I feel like I don't have any energy.

- I'm not really interested in eating.

- Even after a long day, I still feel restless.

- I feel so indecisive and I can't make any decisions.

- I just feel so worthless (Eli Lilly and Company, 2015).

In 2012, I had the privilege of becoming a grandfather for the first time. The hospital gave my daughter a parenting booklet on how to keep babies safe. Some of these safety measures for newborns can be applied – with some modification, mostly tongue-in-cheek – for parents of adult children.

1. **Never shake a newborn:** Never shake your adult child. You may become frustrated with their lack of motivation in seeking employment, self-improvement or implementing new ways of making decisions, but never shake, criticize or belittle them.

2. **Do not give your newborn honey:** Do not give your adult children money. It is a privilege to help your adult children move toward their future and additional money can open many pathways. Cash is often a wonderful blessing to them. However, many adult children will not learn to live on budgets or make wise financial decisions if they are given money to meet wants

or desires rather than essentials, such as insurance, paying down debts or car repairs.

Sibling Relationships

Younger siblings may display a wide range of emotions upon their older brother or sister's return to the home. Parents can create supportive environments for younger siblings by discussing the reasons, goals and benefits of having adult children back in your home such as paying off debt, saving money, getting out of an unhealthy relationship or returning to college.

Siblings need to understand how to be supportive of their older brothers or sisters who return home. Be sure to recognize any sacrifices or inconveniences required of younger siblings upon the return of older brothers or sisters, such as moving to another bedroom or sharing rooms.

Friendships with Our Adult Children

For many parents, the concept of friendships with adult children will be a welcome ideal, but making it happen may seem elusive. My family of origin did not model values such as friendship between parents and children. I am a child of divorce who visited his biological father during summer months.

The relationship with my biological father never developed into a friendship, primarily due to the absence of meaningful experiences. Our relationship developed over events such as vacations and short visits. Relationships that form over events and activities rather than getting to know each other through good times and bad are extremely underdeveloped. We did not have enough time or opportunities to develop a rhythm of life with each other.

Fortunately, my stepdad walked through the normal routines of life with me. However, he did not know how to develop a spiritual identity with me. He was supportive and involved, but unfamiliar with Christianity. Yet his role as a coach in my life was invaluable. I learned to excel in athletics, develop a strong work ethic, gained mechanical skills, and enjoyed hunting and fishing through my relationship with him.

My wife's father died when she was two years old and her mother raised six children as single parent. Her family of origin was also underdeveloped in the areas of friendship.

As a couple, we diligently worked through the deficits in our family of origins in order to establish our own family values such as faith, fun and sacrificial love. We were blessed with a daughter and son who are two years apart. My wife coached our daughter's high school volleyball team, and my son and I were active in sports and outdoor activities.

I began to think about developing friendships with our adult children as they went off to college, but I lacked any personal experiences with a father figure as a friend after I was nineteen years of age. I was at a disadvantage, so I had to do a lot of experimenting.

As our children approached adulthood, we enjoyed budding friendships with them. Barbara and I were clueless about how to develop friendships with them. However, most of the components of friendship were already in place. We had history, good times, difficult times, mutual respect and spiritual values.

I learned that my adult children did not really know me as a friend. One of the first hurdles that you must overcome in order to form friendships with adult children is to break out of parental expectations. My children were locked into a particular father image of me. Most of our shared activities were initiated by me or my wife.

In order to foster change, I began to look for ways to enter into their worlds. I paid attention to what they enjoyed, such as Frisbee golf, music, movies and designer clothes. I let them know that I would like to listen to some of their music, eat at restaurants they preferred or try activities that they enjoyed. It was not long before I was invited along.

The best thing about joining your children's activities, areas of interests or expertise is that they are more skilled and knowledgeable than you. As dads, you are used to winning. However, in their activities, you lose.

Parents benefit from building friendships with adult children. They learn about computers, apps, online shopping, networking, fantasy sports, music, movies and the people who star in them. Adult children play important roles as educators on the genres of young adult culture that would otherwise be inaccessible to parents.

Possible hurdles to friendships occur as children make choices or embrace values that differ from established family values they grew up with, such as drinking alcohol, going to sports bars or night clubs, dating someone of a different culture or ethnicity, or acquiring debt much earlier in life, such as purchasing new cars rather than used ones, wearing designer clothes, etc.

Parents must avoid being judgmental toward adult children as they make choices based upon cultural values and Christian liberties that may challenge the holiness teaching of churches in past generations. Your children may choose to drink beer or wine with dinner, even though alcohol was never present in your home. Legalized marijuana is breaking onto the scene and increasingly, cohabiting couples fit easily into congregational life.

Barbara and I discussed our choice to abstain from alcohol when our children were adolescents. I had to trust that our children would always be wise enough to not abuse alcohol when they reached adulthood. At first, they chose to abstain from drinking alcohol when eating at restaurants with us. Especially if I was buying. However, abstaining from alcohol at dinner was more about not wanting to fail or disappoint us as parents rather than an expression of choice or Christian liberty. As they matured, drinking alcohol was not associated with poor behavior or appearing ungodly, but believing that drinking with boundaries was the best way to show respect for our personal choices and values.

In order to enter their worlds, we initiated conversations about beer or wine and offered to pay for it at restaurants. We did not want our personal preference, of abstaining from alcohol, to get in the way of our growing friendships. I never wanted my children to feel judged for their choices or preferences.

A few years ago, our adult children traveled with us to the island of Maui. On New Year's Eve, they wanted to go to a sports bar to ring in the New Year. My son asked if I would have a beer with him. I said, "Sure."

I was surprised to hear him say later that afternoon, "That didn't seem right, Dad."

He understood that I did not judge him for his choices, but he did not need me to drink a beer in order to be an equal with him. Fortunately, the Scriptures give us liberty to either abstain from or to drink alcohol in moderation.

I was intrigued by the thought of spending an extended amount time with my son, who was twenty-eight at the time. I planned a business trip to Australia and invited him to go along. Fortunately, we both had accumulated enough air miles over the years to pay for airfare. I had two days of work and ten days of free time. It was important to break away from the familiar activities that typically connected us to each other. We were about to experience life as two men simply making their way around Australia.

Our trip started off with a fourteen-hour flight in economy class. My hope was to understand each other more fully and to create shared experiences that would foster greater depth of friendship between us. We decided that plans were stupid, so we planned only one event over the ten days, scuba diving on the Great Barrier Reef. Everything else would be done on a whim. We would wake up and say: "What do you want to do?"

This trip was about two men learning to lead and follow in concert with each other, because parental preferences were out the window. This trip was not about father and son roles, but about two friends who happened to be a father and son traveling around Australia. We had new experiences mixed with fun and stressful moments. Most of the stress was due to shared driving responsibilities in a country where driving on the left side of the road is the norm.

Over the twelve days, we noticed our similarities:

- We both enjoyed the beach for about two hours at a time. After two hours, we were done with the sand and surf.

- We preferred to walk rather than ride in a taxi. We walked between four and six miles a day.

- We equally disliked the exchange rate of $1.11 to one American dollar.

- We both grew to dislike kookaburras that woke us up with their distinct cry at 4:30 a.m. every morning.

- We were more grateful for my wife, because she normally plans all our vacation activities. It is a lot of work trying to figure out what to do without a plan.

- We were both glad to get back to the States to get away from high food and transportation costs.

- We both recognize that God reveals his character and nature through creation.

Some of our differences included:

- I wake up early. My son likes to sleep late.

- I am willing to spend whatever it takes to enjoy a good meal. My son thinks that expensive meals are a poor use of money.

- A fun trip to me is eating local cuisine. My son prefers familiar foods, such as pizza and Taco Bell.

- I am not very moody. My son holds onto moods longer.

- I do not read maps well. My son is an excellent map reader.

- I will turn around after missing a turn. My son wants to find alternate routes rather than turning around.

We truly have the stuff that makes up friendships.

Exercise

Identify the similarities and differences between you and your adult child.

Similarities	Differences

Discussion Questions

1. Identify the benefits that your adult child brings into your relationship.

2. Identify the strengths that you bring into the relationships with your adult child.

3. How can you show appreciation for the benefits that your adult children bring into your life?

4. How do the similarities and differences between you and your adult children affect your relationships, both positively and negatively?

Embrace the Journey

Friendships with adult children do not mean that children and parents will agree on cultural, spiritual or moral values. Friendship is a shared journey of two people committed to form a relationship.

Perhaps the best way to understand friendship is discovered by separating "friend" from "ship." Any two people can choose to become friends. However, they need vehicles to carry them forward on their journey together. The fuel of relationships comes from commitment, sacrifice, love, mutuality, faith or hope. Two people begin a common journey on the ship (catalyst) that forms a new relationship. These vehicles or catalysts can appear in unlikely places and in unchartered waters such as natural disasters, death of family members or social justice issues (hunger in the community). Other vehicles of friendship begin in calmer waters such as mutual enjoyment over golf or other activities.

Friendships with adult children are not based upon parent and child roles, but on learning to relate to each other on a specific journey. The journey may begin as a rescue mission, where parents extend help and encouragement to struggling children. Parents need to look for ships that serve as opportunities for friendship with their adult children. Some of these ships are exciting and welcomed and have mutual benefits, such as sports, hobbies, art or music.

Other catalysts do not have mutual benefits and are difficult to navigate, including out of wedlock pregnancies, drug or alcohol abuse or scholastic struggles. Some parents may miss these types of catalysts of friendship because of their own fear, disappointment, anger or shame. Parents who choose to board these ships may discover that the very crisis that could have driven a wedge between them and their children will serve as the surprising catalysts of lifelong friendships.

Friendship is beautiful but not always easy, convenient or always mutually beneficial. However, friendship has the power to enhance your life in ways that could never be experienced in other environments. In all friendships, there are elements of risks and rewards. Even when friendships end abruptly or painfully, there is still the chance that each person can discover something about him or herself, both positives and negatives. People learn how to be resilient, sacrificial, give up control or be hopeful. At other times, friendships allow you to embrace opportunities to learn more about sacrificial love, extending grace or needing to form healthy boundaries. Walking out friendship will always have the potential to lead to self-discovery that draws you deeper into maturity of faith and life.

I believe that one of the key elements of forming friendships with adult children requires parents to see these relationships as missional opportunities to demonstrate love, grace, mercy and justice. Every follower of Jesus is on mission to demonstrate the love, mercy, grace, righteousness, justice and forgiveness of God to the world. Parents have unique opportunities to include their children in this mission.

Prayer for Parents

Father, I ask that you fill each parent with power, hope and endurance to guide their children into adulthood. I ask the Holy Spirit to reveal the mystery and depths of God's love for them as they parent their fallen but unique and one-of-a-kind children. May your hope, joy and peace fill their hearts. I am confident that you will draw their children into your great salvation and grace. In the name of Jesus, Amen.

Parent Plan

Child's name: _____

Relational contexts: Using the table below, identify at least three relational contexts that your child needs to experience in your home.

Time alone	Needs to feel connected/physical touch
Communicates through questions	Communicates through interacting with parents
Goal/challenge oriented	Rules/structure oriented
Logical	Needs to express emotions

_____   _____   _____

How does your child respond to nurture?

What values will you model to your child, such as communication, time management, respect, etc.

Discipline: Identify preferred methods of discipline to be used to bring your child to repentance for his/her attitudes or behaviors by numbering the options in the table below first, second, third, etc.

	Time out		Logical/natural consequences		Spanking (last resort – never more than two swats)
__	Time out	__	Logical/natural consequences	__	Spanking (last resort – never more than two swats)
__	Behavior modification	__	Choice of consequences	__	Verbal correction

__	Positive redirection	__	Restriction/loss of privileges	__	Other_____

List at least five positive characteristics (bents) of the child.

_____   _____   _____

_____   _____   _____

List at least three negative characteristics (bents) of the child.

_____   _____   _____

Identify any struggles with the following negative emotions. Identify the source/events that generate these emotions:

__	Fear	__	Anger	__	Rejection	__	Other_____
__	Shame	__	Bitterness	__	Separation anxiety	__	Other_____

Identify how your child responds to loss or crisis:

__	Denial	__	Anger	__	Bargaining	__	Depression

What areas of your child's life need prayer? Agree to spend time praying over these areas:

_____   _____   _____

Your child's love language (What is most important to your child?)

_	Time	_	Gifts	_	Service	_	Words of affirmation	_	Physical touch

Completed Parent Plan

You have an eight-year-old son. He feels safest when he has space to do things on his own. He often communicates by asking questions, likes to have a goal to reach, and is very systematic. He tends to do best when family rules are posted. He expresses his emotions through a wide spectrum, from anger to joy to melancholy. He typically avoids conflict. The most effective discipline for him seems to be time outs, verbal correction and natural consequences. His positive characteristics are: compassion, serving others and does well in school. His negative characteristics are: self-criticism, becomes angry when things do not go his way and procrastination. He responds to losses by bargaining and sometimes depression. His primary love language is words of affirmation, with physical touch as his secondary love language. As parents you will pray regularly for him to overcome anger and self-criticism.

Bibliography

Agence France-Presse. (2012, August 8). "Most Young Adults Expect Marriage For Life: Study." Retrieved from Raw Story: http://www.rawstory.com/2012/08/most-young-adults-expect-marriage-for-life-study/

Balswick, J. O. (2003). *Relationship-empowerment Parenting: Building Formative and Fulfilling Relationships with Your Children.* Grand Rapids: Baker Books.

Balswick, J. O. & Balswick, J. K. (2014). *The Family: A Christian Perspective on the Contemporary Home.* Grand Rapids: Baker Academic.

Benner, S. (2002). *Sacred Companions: The Gift of Spiritual Friendship & Direction.* Downers Grove: InterVarsity Press.

Carnevale, A. P., Hanson, A. R. & Gulish, A. (2013, September). *Failure to Launch: Structural Shift and the New Lost Generation.* Washington, DC: Georgetown University Center on Education and the Workforce and The Generations Initiative. Retrieved from: https://cew.georgetown.edu/wp-content/uploads/2014/11/FTL_FullReport.pdf

Cherlin, A. (2010). *The Marriage-Go-Round: The State of Marriage and the Family in America Today.* New York: Vintage Books.

Cohn, D. (2013, February 13). "Love and Marriage." Pew Research Center. Retrieved from: http://www.pewsocialtrends.org/2013/02/13/love-and-marriage/

Eli Lilly and Company. (2015). "Cymbalta." Retrieved from: http://www.cymbalta.com/Pages/understandingdepression.aspx?WT.seg_1=MDD&DCSext.ag=Recognize%20Condition&WT.

mc_ID=GGLMDDDepression&WT.srch=1

Foley, E. B. (2003). *Mutuality Matters: Family, Faith and Just Love.* New York: Rowman & Littlefield Publishers.

Friedman, E. H. (1985). *Generation to Generation.* New York: Guilford Press.

Friedman, E. H. (2007). *The Failure of Nerve.* New York: Church Publishing, Inc.

Glenn, N. D. (2005). *With This Ring ... A National Survey on Marriage in America.* Gaithersburg: National Fatherhood Initiative.

Grobman, K. H. (2003–2008). "Diana Baumrind's (1966) Prototypical Descriptions of 3 Parenting Styles." Retrieved from: http://www.devpsy.org/teaching/parent/baumrind_styles.html

Hitchcock, R. R. (2013, May 3). *The Relationship of Friendship and Shared Values to Couple Satisfaction in Premarital and Married Relationships.* Wilmore: Asbury Theological Seminary.

Holeman, S. L. (2008). *Inside The Leader's Head: Unraveling Personal Obstacles to Ministry.* Nashville: Abingdon Press.

Information Please® Database. (2009). "Median Age at First Marriage, 1890–2010." Retrieved from: http://www.infoplease.com/ipa/A0005061.html

Kastner, L. S. & Wyatt, J. (2002). *The Launching Years: Strategies for Parenting for Senior Year to College.* New York: Random House.

Kinlaw, D. (2104, April 5). "The Family: A Sacred Pedagogy." Retrieved from The Francis Asbury Society: http://www.francisasburysociety.com/resources/articles/the-family-sacred-pedagogy/

Lapowsky, I. (2014, March 3). "Why Teens Are the Most Elusive and Valuable Customers in Tech." Retrieved from Inc.: http://www.inc.com/issie-lapowsky/inside-massive-tech-land-grab-teenagers.html

Mather, M. (2010, May). "U.S. Children in Single-mother Families." Population Reference Bureau. Retrieved from: http://www.prb.org/pdf10/single-motherfamilies.pdf

Mather, M. (2011, September). "In U.S., a Sharp Increase in Young Men Living at Home." Population Reference Bureau. Retrieved from: http://www.prb.org/Publications/Articles/2011/us-young-adults-living-at-home.aspx

Merriam-Webster. (2015). "Faithful." Retrieved from: http://www.merriam-webster.com/dictionary/faithful

Merriam-Webster. (2015). "Success." Retrieved from: http://www.merriam-webster.com/dictionary/success

Pew Reseach Center. (2012, October 9). "'Nones' on the Rise." Retrieved from: http://www.pewforum.org/2012/10/09/nones-on-the-rise/

Pope, J. (2012, January 3). "Average Student Loan Debt: $25,250." The Associated Press. Retrieved from: http://www.huffingtonpost.com/2011/11/03/average-student-debt-2525_n_1073335.html

Seligman, M. A. (2000). "Positive Psychology: An Introduction." *American Psychologist* 55.1, 5–14.

Silver-Greenberg, J. (2011, November 26). "When Kids Come Back Home." *The Wall Street Journal.* Retrieved from: http://www.wsj.com/articles/SB10001424052970203710704577054431508215886

Stienke, R. (2006). *How Your Church Family Works.* Herndon: The Alban Institute.

Thompson, M. J. (1998). *Family the Forming Center: A Vision of the Role of Family in Spiritual Formation.* Nashville: Upper Room Books.

Wallerstein, J. S., Lewis, J. M. & Blakeslee, S. (2000). *The Unexpected Legacy of Divorce: A 25 Year Landmark Study.* New York: Hyperion.

Wikipedia. (2015, January 12). "Differentiation of self." Retrieved from: http://en.wikipedia.org/wiki/Murray_Bowen

Wikipedia. (2014, March 8). "Helicopter parent." Retrieved from:

http://en.wikipedia.org/wiki/Helicopter_parent

Wikipedia. (2015, April 14). "*Lectio Divina.*" Retrieved from: http://en.wikipedia.org/wiki/Lectio_Divina

Witty. (2014, March 8). "Vent Quote #5168303." Retrieved from: http://test.wittyprofiles.com/q/5168303

Made in the USA
Charleston, SC
08 September 2015